DOMA

DOMA

Traditional flavors and
modern recipes from the
Balkan diaspora

Spasia Pandora Dinkovski

Contents

A Journey into Burek

The year 2020 was spent missing everything and everyone all at once. The world wrapped itself in silence and I wondered if it was time to open my grandmother, Baba Slavka's, recipe book. As the future looked uncertain, her Gibanica egg and cheese filo pie was the thing I missed the most. I'd request it to greet me at the table anytime I returned to North Macedonia and, sure enough, that's where it would always be, no matter what time I'd arrive from the airport. I'd previously struggled to open the book she'd passed down to me – it was as if I was saving it for a special occasion or fearful of re-living the grief of losing her. Or maybe I was just too busy with that thing we call life.

So eventually I opened my grandmother's cookbook, made her pie, and then started to wonder what other ingredients I could add, how else I could manipulate the pastry, and what experiences of my own I could pour into it before it went in the oven. I made the bold move of spending the very last of my money on ingredients and I posted pictures of my pies to an audience of friends online, who shared it enough that perfect strangers began messaging me, asking how they could buy them.

I never intended to start a business, but it was the correlation between the all-night burek shops (burekdzilnicas) in the Balkans and the pizza-slice shops of Brooklyn, and what they bring to communities, that really got me thinking. So I ordered some food boxes and designed a logo while re-watching *Mystic Pizza* for the millionth time, and lo and behold, Mystic Burek was born.

I baked my pies in a little two-shelf domestic oven at home, selling them via Instagram and delivering them all over London in a little pink trolley until my little Brixton kitchen could take it no more. I moved the business to a rented commercial space, hustling hard and travelling across the city to serve my food at sell-out events; a combination of filo pies and Balkan-British dinners. I fought long and hard to find my own space – a shop in Southeast London – never once stopping for breath; a resilience passed down to me not only by my ancestors but also my parents. Having moved to the UK many moons ago, they committed their lives to the NHS and social care, building a life for me and giving me all I've ever needed along the way – backbone and guts. I built the business all on my own and I thank them endlessly for showing me the value of hard work.

So, what does Mystic Burek mean? Well, it's second-generation Balkan cooking at its finest, using ancient techniques to create something totally new – and yet completely authentic – wrapped up in filo pastry.

At Mystic Burek we make hand-rolled pies that would traditionally come with a choice of meat, cheese, or spinach. These same pies are now filled with combinations such as harissa butter, Bulgarian white cheese and wild garlic, or lamb sausage, confit spring onion and apricots. We also serve old-school snacks, such as Smoki peanut puffs, recognized by those from the former Yugoslavia and loved by all.

"That's not burek", "This is not borek", "Oh, you weren't born there?", "I expected you to have an accent!" are just some of the comments I've received since starting the business. Then there are the miserable guardians of authenticity who are bogged down by being the authority on all that they deem to be black and white, unable to accept the very concept of diaspora cooking, probably as they are just unable to relate. There's enough room at the table for all of us and our varying life experiences.

So to understand me, it's important to have an understanding of what I do. I'm Macedonian, and both my parents were born there. I was, however, born in Crawley, a small, diverse town in West Sussex, and so I'm British too. I spent whole summers back in the Balkans, leaving as soon as school was out and returning just in time for the new school year. I've also lived in New York, and I've worked in countless hot and heavy kitchens, trying my hand at any cuisine that would pay my wages at the time.

The dishes in this book are how I naturally cook; some traditional recipes, some modern dishes, but flavours all within the same dimension. We could call this "fusion food", and "fusion" is appropriate in the right context, embraced by the correct hands. My words are to teach you about Balkan culture, acknowledging and honouring traditions.

One thing is for sure: I can't represent everyone. I'm not a historian and even if I was, there'd be countless people who would disagree with me. I could write this book like a Wikipedia article and give you the various names for each recipe or try to piece together a history that has many questions, with burnt books and papers, torn up by war and political conflict, but somehow that doesn't feel appropriate.

To set the scene, Yugoslavia was a socialist federation made up of Bosnia and Herzegovina, Croatia, North Macedonia, Montenegro, Serbia (including Kosovo and Vojvodina), and Slovenia, and broken up following the war in 1992. Whatever impact socialism, communism, or conflict had on our region, a sense of nostalgia will always remain for that sense of togetherness.

I remember my mum desperately trying to dial my nan's number on one of those phones that lived on the wall, her shaking hands frantically winding the numbers, shortly after hearing news of the first bombs.

The former Yugoslavian countries are who, naturally as a Macedonian, I have the most in common with. We are Balkan, ex-Yugoslavian, South-East European. We speak a Slavic language, and we were occupied by the Ottoman Empire for 500 years, hence the heavy Turkish influence on our cuisines.

As well as the history books that may or may not have been re-written, there are the people. The only real way to understand a culture is by studying how the people live, how they behave, and what they are eating at this very moment in time. I seek to capture a moment, a pivotal point in society where we are seriously faced with the concept of change, of the new, while finding a way to still honour the old, the elders, the ones that got us here.

I suppose I have an advantage being a kid of the diaspora; when something is right in front of you, you might become tired of it, you might spend too much time noticing it becoming uglier, unable to refocus your attention on holding on to the beauty of it. There's a romanticism with me returning "home" to Macedonia when I wasn't physically born there, and my eyes and heart are wide open to all of its endless charm and my attitude is infectious. I excite those that were born there with my never-ending enthusiasm and desperate efforts to honour them, to tell their story.

A common theme that pops up in my conversations is how the concept of home – or "doma" – changes over time. You lose someone and the table becomes less crowded, the room a little quieter and it's as if a little bit of "home" turns into rubble. You may not mention them a million times a day but it's about finding a way to make them proud, and as with cultural traditions, it's a way of doing so that feels organic to you. I'll never lose my grip on tradition, but I've found my own voice that also echoes all of the phone calls to my mum and aunties, asking them to re-explain their recipes.

That said, working on the traditional recipes for this book proved to be the biggest challenge, mainly because many didn't work at first. The oldest would always follow a similar format of feeling like they would probably take all day to prepare and make enough to serve five thousand. This is because they were created by women who would spend all their time at the oven, tending to the meals and cooking for huge families. I also thought it was only my nan who seemed to have left out many crucial steps or ingredients in her recipes (as much as I love her cookbook, it's light on detail), but it turns out to be a very Balkan trait. I wonder if it's because skilled hands only need a brief guide, or is it because the elders secretly don't want you to make anything as good as they could, so that they will always be remembered?

Focusing on the people of a region means we get to really delve into how we like to eat, with lots of garlic and parsley, white cheese, peppers, raw onions, and chunks of bread "za machkenje" to mop it all up. We eat with the seasons and from the markets, full of punchy and simple flavours that hit our tastebuds like a thunderclap. We start our meals with a salad and a shot of something strong, sometimes followed by a broth, then move on to meze before winding through to bigger plates, all savoured for as long as possible – we are champions of how to dine. Our sweet tooths crave cream and walnuts and pots of Eurocrem (similar to Nutella). Within our dimension of flavour sits a core list of ingredients that winds through recipes, and techniques are repeated, born of our frugal ancestors who would create multiple dishes from the same base recipes.

As much as I can cover in this book, I'll never be able to include all the recipes from one region, or document how wildly they differ from town to town, let alone between neighbouring countries. So I've picked my favourites, just how I've always cooked; I make what I want to eat. I'm not sure if you're a middle- or edge-of-the lasagne sort of person but I'm definitely the edge, and when I want pudding, I want something indulgent, no holding back.

Use my serving sizes as a guide, I'm not here to judge. I am here to remind you to taste your food as you cook and let your hands lead you; touch everything as much as possible and work with the environment you are in.

Although I do this for a living, cooking at home is the thing I love to do the most, and just like the people I met while making this book, my story also began at home. How lucky I am that I can say that about two very different places. I spent time back in North Macedonia, devouring young cheeses on a blanket in the middle of nowhere. I also lay under one all night on my sofa in London, writing about those young cheeses. I learnt invaluable recipes from my elders but I also frantically reached for my phone to make notes on ideas for my own dishes, while baking for my business.

It was only in North Macedonia that I came home to the biggest tomato my Aunt Suze could find, picked from the market and left in the fridge as a welcome present, and only in London did I meet so many other second- and third-generation kids who helped me feel more comfortable. The ingredients themselves may never taste quite the same but just as I adapted to feeling more Balkan, the foods we have around us could always be a little more Balkan too.

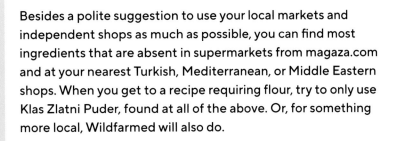

Besides a polite suggestion to use your local markets and independent shops as much as possible, you can find most ingredients that are absent in supermarkets from magaza.com and at your nearest Turkish, Mediterranean, or Middle Eastern shops. When you get to a recipe requiring flour, try to only use Klas Zlatni Puder, found at all of the above. Or, for something more local, Wildfarmed will also do.

For any recipe that calls for brined white cheese, you could always use feta, but if you can, find a sheep's or cow's milk white cheese – there are some seriously delicious Bulgarian ones on the market. If it's ajvar that you need and you don't have time to deal with the peppers, then Mamma's is your best bet. Don't fall for any imitations that are produced outside of the region. I instruct the use of long peppers over bell peppers a lot and it's worth sticking to this. And finally, if it's rakija you are after, then vardar.com or theoldcellar.com is where you should go. Na zdravje!

Зим

Preserves and Condiments

An Orchestra of Hands

There are mystical Macedonian moments occurring throughout the year that pull whole families together, poignant reminders of ancient techniques that revolve around food and capturing the best of the season. The ritual of filling enough tegli (jars) to last throughout the darker months was once essential in harder times, but now pivots more to a pure celebration of tradition, conducted by the older generation and requiring a whole orchestra of helping hands.

The process that practically defines us happens between September and October, when the markets are swollen with huge, juicy red peppers and other fruits and vegetables peacocking their way out of summer. The air smells like it's on fire, and sweet, burning wood and a sense of ritualistic calm falls over the country. Waves of households busy themselves with making zimnica (preserves), all sorts of pickles and sauces but most importantly, ajvar and ljutenica. Both are relish royalty to us, as commonplace as ketchup to others, but on a God-tier level of condiments. Although you can buy both in supermarkets all over the world now, there's no denying that homemade will always be the best. As with many recipes there is open debate as to where these originate from; they're deeply loved Balkan-wide but it's commonly agreed that there's something special about the peppers in Serbia and North Macedonia.

I spent the day at Vera's house in Skopje, a house that has been making both relishes in the exact same way for 50 years from recipes passed down by her mum, Baba Danica. It was a legacy I could feel as soon as I stepped through the garden gate. A burst of warmth and welcome but also a silent hum of seriousness as they embark on this very important task. Today we're making ljutenica, and from the second I sat down at Vera's table, I realized that this house is a pillar of the community with a carousel of neighbours leaning over the gate – local bonds that have lasted a lifetime. I knew that this family was infamous for honouring this time of year.

Before we began making the relishes, I quickly found myself surrounded by jars, spoons, bottles, and pickles, all brought out for me to try. It's so common for us to show off what we've made to our guests, bombarding them with our latest recipes for rum liquor with plums or rakija with walnuts, and last year's ajvar. A trip for the senses and the fastest route to the feeling of home.

Everyone had their own role to take responsibility for, and Vera told me that she had inspected every pepper that would be used, made sure the jars were are all spotless, and personally snipped away with scissors at the parsley. She talked to me about her job as president of the local women's rights organization, and her time as a professor of geography – a powerhouse of a woman. She clearly knows that taking your time over something, putting the effort in and working with meaning, will produce the best and the most long-lasting results, ensuring the preserves remain just as perfect all year round.

Jane (Yaaneh), Vera's nephew, brought in 40kg (88lb) of peppers, lit the wood fire and spent hours slowly roasting each one, turning them by hand and then throwing them into a bag that is then sealed so that the skins start to steam, making it easier (but never that easy) to remove the bitter char. Jane is the king of peppers – the company he owns even produces the giant pot that he stood over – and he was so animated when he talked about the tradition of making the relish. It was obvious that this meant a lot to him, to come here every year and live out his passion with explosive pride.

Peeling the peppers is when everyone else gets involved – a long table of family, huddled over bags of peppers and bowls of water to keep their hands clean, hours of conversation and peeling, hands wet and starting to wrinkle, backs hurting, rakija pouring, spirits rising and Turkish coffee brewing for breaks.

The next day each pepper is sliced and added to the giant pot, and this time Jane has his apron on and bears a giant paddle-like wooden spoon, embarking on a full afternoon of constant stirring, slowly adding oil then garlic, followed by hot peppers, salt, and parsley, and then more stirring. It makes sense to me that he used to work in an army kitchen; his physical energy for this task comes

from training, but it's also clear that it's his love for Vera that pushes him to strive for perfection.

Once the ljutenica is ready, he grabs the huge pot and gracefully takes it to the kitchen where they join forces. Vera fills the jars and Jane seals them, a waltz full of so much respect for each other I start to well-up. In our current climate of no one ever having enough time, how fulfilling this dance must be, how crucial it feels to hold on to a whole weekend of working hard on something special together. It makes me want to start my own traditions to honour my ancestors as our elders start to slip away.

We finish by each grabbing a chunk of bread to mop up the warm relish from the bottom of the pot. The obsessive stirring means the texture is the same throughout, nothing has caught on the bottom, and the hyper level of care washes over me with every flawless bite. Jane's face looks like it's going to split open with happiness as he sees my reaction and notices the tears in my eyes as I'm gushing over how much work has gone into this, and how tired they must be. As I leave, they tell me that next weekend they'll do the same with aubergines (eggplant) to make a big batch of malidzano, another laborious dance that holds them so tightly together.

Ljutenica

As with many of my recipes, I've adapted this spicy red pepper relish (pronounced "lyootenitsa") to suit the ingredients I had to hand. The red peppers may not taste the same as those used in the traditional recipe, and the small hot green peppers may be slightly different, but this is still delicious. Serious commitment should be given to the stirring – you can taste the level of care.

Be like Vera (see page 16) and inspect the vegetables in the shop or at the market for any mould or bruising, so you know you'll be preserving the best on offer when you get home. The peppers can be charred up to a day in advance if you want to get ahead.

To sterilize the jars, either run the opened jars and lids through the dishwasher on the hottest setting or submerge them in a large pan of water and boil for 10 minutes. Allow to air dry rather than drying with a tea towel.

MAKES ABOUT 1 LITRE (1¾ PINTS)

12 sweet, red pointed peppers (such as Romano)

2 large tomatoes

200ml (7fl oz) vegetable oil

30ml (1fl oz) white wine vinegar

1 tbsp caster (superfine) sugar

6 small, hot green chillies

½ bunch of parsley, roughly chopped

3 garlic cloves, roughly chopped

Char the peppers by carefully holding them over the flames of a gas hob, or under a grill (broiler) heated to the highest setting, turning often, until almost entirely blackened but still with a little bite. Immediately transfer to a plastic bag or large plastic container with a lid, sealing the bag or closing the lid after each addition – this will make the peeling process easier. Leave the peppers in the sealed bag or covered container for about an hour or set aside until the following day.

Meanwhile, add the tomatoes to a pan of water. Bring to the boil over a medium heat and cook for 15 minutes or until the tomatoes have softened and their skins have started to burst. Drain and set aside. Once cool enough to handle, peel away the skins and discard, then add the flesh to a blender or food processor and blend until chunky. Set aside.

Half fill a large bowl with water. Remove the peppers from the bag or container and carefully remove the charred skins, discarding them and dipping your hands in the water as you go to clean them. Deseed and roughly chop the peppers.

Heat a splash of the oil in a large saucepan over a low heat. Add the peppers, vinegar, sugar, and tomatoes. Cook for 10 minutes, stirring continuously to prevent the mixture from catching.

Add the remaining oil a little at a time, stirring between each addition, then continue to cook on low for 30 minutes, stirring frequently.

Add the chillies, parsley, and garlic and continue to cook for a further 15 minutes, stirring frequently. Allow to cool and store in the fridge for up to 2 weeks in a sealed container or for up to 6 months in a sterilized jar.

Slatko – Tikva

Although traditionally made with pumpkin, this quick, delicious, stripped-back recipe is for preserved squash, as squash is more readily available and doesn't need soaking. Slatko literally means sweet, but it's also used to describe anything that has been preserved in a thick syrup.

A month before I was born, my grandmother, Baba Slavka, arrived in the UK to await the newest arrival to the family. She brought an array of treats with her – such as small ornate cakes and snacks that Mum and Dad had been missing. But the most important thing she brought (or rather dragged, through airports and up goodness knows how many flights of stairs) was a 5-litre (1-gallon) tub of candied pumpkin and grapes. She even brought her favourite silver tray, a glass dish, her best gold spoons, and a crystal water glass – when it came to hospitality, she strived for perfection. The first time the midwife came to visit, my grandmother opened the door and greeted her with a tray of treats – a surprising custom, I'm sure, but a nice one at that.

The sweetness of the slatko is to make guests feel welcome and the water is to refresh them. I can only imagine how important it felt to my grandmother to honour the person who had come to check on her precious grandchild. So important, in fact, that she spent the next seven days standing in the kitchen, watching like a hawk from the window whenever the midwife was due. And as soon as she saw the navy cape drifting round the corner, there she was proud and ready at the door with her silver tray.

I use this recipe for my twist on Nafora on page 49, but you can serve it with granola or porridge, as part of a cheese board or even on a fancy silver tray, with a golden spoon and a crystal glass.

MAKES 1 LITRE (1¾ PINTS)

500g (1lb 2oz) caster (superfine) sugar

Juice of 2 lemons

1kg (2¼lb) butternut squash, peeled, deseeded and chopped into 5cm (2in) cubes

Combine the sugar, lemon juice, and 120ml (4fl oz) water in a large saucepan over a medium heat. Bring to a simmer and stir slowly until the sugar has dissolved.

Add the squash and reduce the heat to low. Allow to simmer, covered, for 40 minutes.

Remove the lid and continue to cook for 2 hours or until the syrup has the consistency of honey.

Cool thoroughly before serving. Store in the fridge for up to 2 weeks in a sealed container, or for up to 6 months in a sterilized jar (see page 21).

Slatko – Kora od Lubenica

It gets really hot in North Macedonia, the kind of heat that wraps around you like a heavy blanket, forcing mid-afternoon naps and al fresco dinners at 10pm. This must be where the fascination with watermelon comes from, cooling you down like no other nectar on earth. And this recipe (pronounced "kora od lubenitsa") for preserved watermelon rind in syrup (slatko literally translates as "sweet") makes use of the bit that is usually discarded.

I remember standing on our balcony back home, watching the trailer of melons bouncing along the street, pulling up below me and eagerly awaiting whoever volunteered to go downstairs and tap each one to find the winning fruit. We'd bide our time listening for the doorbell or heavy footsteps on the stairs because, if the watermelon was big enough, the sellers would bring it all the way up for you. My mum or nan would then cut into the sweet juicy fruit and rip it open – I'll never forget the moment everyone cheered as the deep, crimson colour was revealed, giving them the satisfaction of knowing that they'd selected the best fruit for us all. This recipe is ancient, and you can tell by its philosophy: why waste good food?

MAKES 1 LITRE (1¾ PINTS)

1 medium watermelon

150ml (5fl oz) white wine vinegar

About 1kg (2¼lb) caster (superfine) sugar (you may not need all of it)

Juice of 2 lemons

Cut the ends of the watermelon and peel away the tough, green skin.

Cut the watermelon into 8 pieces and carefully remove the rind, leaving about 1cm (½in) of the red flesh attached. Try to do this as evenly as possible to ensure all the pieces cook at the same time, either by trimming as you go or by cutting the slices into smaller chunks.

You should now have about 850g (1¾lb) of rind, give or take 250g (9oz). Either slice the rind into 5cm (2in) chunks or thin slices.

Pour 1.5 litres (2¾ pints) of water into a large saucepan over a medium heat and add the vinegar. Bring to the boil, carefully add the rind and allow to simmer for about an hour, then remove from the heat and allow to cool.

Drain the cooled rind, gently pressing out any excess liquid and taking care not to damage the flesh. Weigh the rind and then weigh out an equal quantity of sugar.

Rinse the saucepan and add the sugar along with 300ml (10fl oz) water. Place over a medium heat until the sugar has dissolved, then add the rind and lemon juice. Continue to cook for 40 minutes or until the mixture forms a light syrup.

Store in the fridge for up to 14 days in a sealed container, or for 8–12 months in a sterilized jar (see page 21). Serve with Crispy White Fish (see page 126), on thick, buttered toast, or as part of a cheese board with creamy cheeses or fried halloumi.

Sweet Tea Pickles

Well, it would have been strange to not include a nod to a decent cup of tea in this book! I'm fully trained in making several at once, each one differing in strength or sweetness, depending on the request. Teatime is a ritual my family grew into as the young ones started to become more British in their habits and needs. The love of tea spans borders and cultures – a symbol of time, I always think, stopping you in your tracks to brew the perfect cuppa. The ritual of stopping for tea has been lost over time, as life has become too busy.

It's best to make this a day ahead so that the tea bag can sit in the liquid and infuse properly.

MAKES 1 LITRE (1¾ PINTS)

500g (1lb 2oz) caster (superfine) sugar

300ml (10fl oz) white wine vinegar

5 English breakfast teabags

800g (1¾lb) mixed vegetables, such as red onions and carrots

3 tbsp salt

Add the sugar and vinegar to a large saucepan. Add the teabags and bring to the boil, then remove from the heat and allow to cool completely before setting aside in the fridge overnight.

The following day, peel and roughly chop the vegetables and place into a colander set over a bowl. Cover the vegetables with the salt and leave for 1–4 hours to allow the excess water to drain.

Transfer the vegetables to an airtight container or sterilized jar (see page 21). Remove the teabags from the vinegar mixture and pour the liquid over the vegetables, making sure they are fully submerged. The pickles will be ready to eat in 3 days and can be stored in the fridge for up to 2 weeks in an airtight container or 6 months in a sterilized jar.

Ajvar

From the Turkish word "havyar" and the Persian "xaviyar", which are both used to describe caviar, the name "ajvar" represents just how precious this red pepper and aubergine relish (pronounced "ayvaar") is to all from the former Yugoslavia.

As with other traditional recipes, it's so routinely made and eaten that we could all argue until we are blue in the face as to how you should make it. Should you use aubergine? How long should you cook it for? How much oil goes in? Most people from former Yugoslavian countries make it and almost all of them will tell you that theirs is the best. I find it funny how easy it is to argue these things and to miss the point that if something has been made a billion times by millions of people, how can there not be variations and how can we truly know which recipe for ajvar should rule them all?

As with the Ljutenica (see page 21), I've gone for the time-saving route that requires a little less effort and in much smaller quantities but still evokes the same feelings of dipping fresh bread into the bottom of the pot and falling so in love with it, you'll make sure it's always on the table.

MAKES 1 LITRE (1¾ PINTS)

12 sweet, red pointed peppers (such as Romano)

3 aubergines (eggplant)

50ml (1¾fl oz) vegetable or sunflower oil

7 garlic cloves, finely chopped

3 tbsp white wine vinegar or apple cider vinegar

Salt

Char the peppers and aubergines by carefully holding them over the flames of a gas hob, or under a grill (broiler) heated to the highest setting, turning often, until almost entirely blackened. Both the peppers and the aubergines should be softened but the peppers should still have a little bite. Immediately transfer to a plastic bag or large plastic container with a lid, sealing the bag or closing the lid after each addition – this will make the peeling process easier. Leave in the sealed bag or container for about an hour or set aside until the following day.

Half fill a large bowl with water. Remove the peppers and aubergines from the bag or container and carefully remove the charred skins, discarding the skins and dipping your hands in the water as you go to clean them. Deseed the peppers and roughly chop both the peppers and aubergines.

Transfer the chopped vegetables to a blender or food processor and briefly blitz. Alternatively chop by hand into super-fine chunks. Set aside.

Add a splash of the oil to a large non-stick saucepan over a low heat and gently fry the garlic until softened. Add the vegetables and bring to a gentle boil over a medium heat, then reduce the heat to low. Cook for 15 minutes, stirring continuously to prevent the mixture from catching and using a spatula to scrape down the sides of the pan.

Add half the oil and cook for 15 minutes, then add the remaining oil, vinegar, and a pinch of salt and cook for a further 15 minutes, or until the mixture has reduced and a thin layer of oil has formed on top.

Store in the fridge for up to 14 days in a sealed container, or for 8–12 months in a sterilized jar (see page 21).

Green Tomato Hot Sauce

Green tomatoes are a much overlooked delicacy – crunchy, tart, fabulously shiny, and available all year round. You can find them at most farmers' markets during early autumn; if you can't spot them then ask the sellers if they can source them for you.

Markets are a whole culture of their own in the Balkans, and where you shop if you're smart. If you know who's selling the best produce, that's whose house you want to eat at. So do the same and make friends with the people who work at your local market, they are your connections to the magical world of fruit and veg – support them and keep their culture alive. Make this hot sauce, take some to the market trader to say thank you, then come home and slather it on eggs, steak, grilled cheese sandwiches... you catch my drift.

MAKES 1.5 LITRES (2¾ PINTS)

3 tbsp salt

1kg (2¼lb) green tomatoes, destemmed

75ml (2½fl oz) vegetable or sunflower oil

5 green bird's eye chillies

1 bunch of spring onions (scallions)

2 handfuls of parsley

8 garlic cloves

80g (2¾oz) sugar

500ml (16fl oz) white wine vinegar

Pour 1 litre (1¾ pints) water into a large saucepan and add 1 tbsp of the salt. Bring to the boil over a medium heat and add the tomatoes. Boil for 12 minutes or until the skins of the tomatoes start to crack. Drain the tomatoes and allow to cool.

Gently peel the skins away from the tomatoes and discard. Add the peeled tomatoes to a blender or food processer with the remaining ingredients. Blitz until smooth.

Pour the mixture back into the saucepan and return to a medium heat. Bring to the boil, then reduce the heat to low and cook for about 30 minutes, stirring occasionally to ensure the sugar dissolves and to prevent the mixture from catching.

Store in the fridge for up to 14 days in a sealed container or for 8–12 months in a sterilized jar (see page 21). Goes well with hardboiled eggs or Fried Chicken with Kaçamak (see page 180).

Pomegranate Hot Sauce

Pomegranates, or as we call them, kalinki, are practically idolized in North Macedonia and have become symbolic across the region. I echo members of my paternal family, who all find it hard to adjust from picking them off their own trees and struggle to find the same level of sweetness in those little jewels in the UK. If you're UK-based, your best bet is to buy them when they are in season from late summer to early winter from Mediterranean or Middle Eastern supermarkets, usually piled high in crates outside and on special offer. Using a good molasses can render results that are just as good, and this fruity and bold hot sauce is proof of just that.

Biber salcasi is a rich, red pepper paste you can find in any Mediterranean supermarket or online retailers.

MAKES ABOUT 1 LITRE (1¾ PINTS)

50ml (1¾fl oz) vegetable or sunflower oil

300g (10oz) biber salcasi

4 garlic cloves, finely chopped

3 small red bird's eye chillies, blended or very finely chopped

350g (12oz) pomegranate molasses

6 tbsp caster (superfine) sugar

1 tbsp chilli flakes

1 tbsp sumac

1 tbsp salt

Heat a splash of the oil in a large non-stick saucepan over a low heat. Add the biber salcasi and garlic along with a splash of water and cook for about 10 minutes, stirring occasionally.

Add the remaining ingredients along with 400ml (14fl oz) water and increase the heat to medium. Bring to a rolling boil and then reduce the heat to low. Cook for 30 minutes, stirring occasionally.

Store in the fridge for up to 14 days in a sealed container or for 8–12 months in a sterilized jar (see page 21).

Green Pepper Jam

Many recipes call for long, sweet peppers, but regular bell peppers are celebrated here, their crunch immortalized in this preserve. Use this any way you like; scoop it onto a big chunk of Cheddar, preferably using a butter knife for both so the chunk becomes a wedge and you keep wanting to add more of this moreish jam.

MAKES 400G (14OZ)

4 green bell peppers
2 jalapeños
200g (7oz) caster (superfine) sugar
200ml (7floz) white wine vinegar
80ml (2¾fl oz) liquid pectin
Salt

Add the peppers and Jalapeños to a blender or food processer and pulse until finely chopped.

Transfer the chopped peppers and Jalapeños to a large saucepan over a medium heat. Add the sugar, vinegar and salt to taste. Bring to the boil and cook for 5 minutes, stirring occasionally.

Add the pectin, stir to combine and cook for a further 5 minutes.

Skim the foam off the top of the mixture and set aside to cool. The jam will be ready to use in 24 hours.

Store in an airtight container in the fridge for up to 4 weeks or in a sterilized jar (see page 21) for up to 6 months.

Makalo

If you don't like garlic then this book may not be for you, and if you're really into it then there's a great chance that you'll be into Balkan cooking. The word makalo (pronounced "makahlo") is derived from the Macedonian word meaning "to dip". The most popular version is made with vezeni piperki – a type of pepper. Vezeni translates to "embroidered" and they are given this name as their skin looks as if it has been sewn all over. These peppers are native to North Macedonia, and are also known as the rheza pepper. They are hung out to dry and then combined with lots of garlic and oil and usually served with boiled potatoes. I am unable to buy those sweet peppers in the UK and I've long since run out of the last big bag I stuffed into my suitcase, but this spread still hits the right notes, like a tangy, funky butter. It works particularly well as a base for cold cuts or in a pickle sandwich.

MAKES 200G (7OZ)

2 garlic cloves

150g (5½oz) butter at room temperature

2¾ tbsp white wine vinegar or apple cider vinegar

Chopped parsley, to serve

Blend the garlic and butter together in a blender or food processor until smooth.

Slowly add the vinegar, a splash at a time, continuing to blend as if you were making mayonnaise. This will allow the vinegar and fat to emulsify.

Store in an airtight container for up to 5 days. Bring back to room temperature any time you want to eat it and serve with plenty of chopped parsley.

Photographed centre left on page 35.

Tomato Jam

Preserving tomatoes is straightforward according to my aunties and many others; you simply roast them, peel them, blitz them and pour them into a jar, eternalizing them in peak summer or, better still, right at the end of the season when the flesh turns into a super-sweet jelly. You can then use the jars for the rest of the year's cooking, or simply down the sweet tomato preserve as an au naturel smoothie.

Make this jam in summer when tomatoes are at their best and use it to accompany the Fried Green Tomatoes on page 134, or in any situation that calls for an equally sweet and savoury spread. The oil that sits on the top can be used for an extra special green salad like the one on page 108.

MAKES ABOUT 1.3KG (2¾LB)

1kg (2¼lb) ripe tomatoes

2 medium onions

2 garlic cloves

2 tbsp smoked paprika

200ml (7fl oz) vegetable or sunflower oil

200g (7oz) caster (superfine) sugar

150ml (5fl oz) white wine vinegar

About 1 tbsp salt, or to taste

Place the tomatoes in a large saucepan and cover with water. Bring to the boil over a medium heat and cook for 15 minutes or until the tomatoes have softened and their skins have started to burst. Drain and set aside to cool.

Add the tomatoes to a blender or food processor along with the remaining ingredients, reserving a little of the salt. Blend until smooth, then transfer the mixture to a large non-stick saucepan over a medium heat.

Bring to the boil, then turn to the lowest heat and cook for around 2 hours, stirring occasionally and scraping down the sides with a spatula as the mixture reduces, until the jam is sticky, smooth and darkened in colour. Taste and add the remaining salt if needed.

Store in an airtight container in the fridge for up to 4 weeks or in a sterilized jar (see page 21) for up to 6 months.

Photographed centre right on page 34.

Tursija

This is a classic way of pickling vegetables; you can use almost any vegetables in this recipe (pronounced "toorshiya") and enjoy them all year round, although traditionally the pickles are reserved for the dead of winter to accompany that all-important pre-dinner shot and salad. They're light and refreshing and it's of utmost importance to only use the most perfect and in-season vegetables. I'm using cauliflower here, which is available in the UK all year round, but the taste and size tend to be best from early summer to mid-autumn.

You can easily gauge how many jars you need once you've portioned your vegetables up, but I used three 1 litre (1¾ pint) jars.

MAKES 3 LITRES (5¼ PINTS)

700ml (24fl oz) white wine vinegar

12 dried bay leaves

12 garlic cloves

2 tbsp salt

250ml (9fl oz) vegetable oil

2 large cauliflowers, broken
 into florets

Pour 2 litres (3½ pints) water into a large saucepan and add the vinegar, bay leaves, garlic, salt, and oil. Bring to the boil over a medium heat and stir to combine until the salt has dissolved.

Turn off the heat and add the cauliflower. Tightly cover the pan with cling film (plastic wrap) and cover with the lid. Set aside for 8–12 hours.

Remove the cauliflower, bay leaves, and garlic from the pan using a slotted spoon and decant into the sterilized jars. Pour over the pickling liquid and seal the jars tightly. The pickles will be ready to eat in 4 days and can be stored in the fridge in a sterilized jar (see page 21) for up to 6 months.

Photographed bottom left on page 34.

Preserved Lemon and Garlic Crispy Chilli Oil

Although preserved lemons aren't the most traditional ingredient in Balkan cuisine, when you share so many recipes with other cultures, it's easy to play around with ingredient combinations and create a new generation in the art of flavour matching. I've served this oil with my filo (phyllo) pastry pies many times and sold out of it as a product in its own right many more times – you will be hard pushed to find a savoury dish in this book that doesn't taste good covered in this.

The corn should stay crispy for up to seven days once added to the oil. If you're planning on storing the oil for longer, store the crushed corn in a separate airtight container and add to the oil just before serving.

MAKES ABOUT 800ML (1½ PINTS)

150g (5½oz) dried crispy corn, salted or chilli and lime flavoured

10 garlic cloves

500ml (16fl oz) vegetable, sunflower or rapeseed (canola) oil

3 preserved lemons

3 tbsp chilli flakes

2 tbsp smoked paprika

2 tsp salt

Add the corn to a blender or food processor and pulse until roughly chopped. (I always do this first as just a tiny drop of liquid in the blender will make the corn soggy.) Transfer to an airtight container and set aside.

Place the garlic in a small saucepan over the lowest heat and cover with 200ml (7fl oz) of the oil. Cook the garlic for about 15 minutes or until it's soft but not crispy, using tongs to turn the cloves and to gently test their softness. Set aside to cool.

Transfer the garlic to the blender or food processor with a little oil from the pan (reserve the remaining oil) and the preserved lemons, and blend until completely smooth.

Transfer the garlic and lemon purée to a non-stick frying pan over a low heat. Add the chilli, paprika, and salt and gently fry for 8 minutes, stirring constantly. Add the remaining oil and the reserved oil from the pan. Remove from the heat and allow to cool.

If you are planning on using the oil within 7 days, add the corn and whisk to combine. If not, store the corn in a separate airtight container and add just before serving.

Pour the oil into a sterilized bottle (see page 21) and refrigerate. The oil will be ready to use the next day and can be stored in the fridge for up to 14 days. Remember to give it a good shake before serving.

Photographed top left on page 35.

Hibiscus Pickles with Pistachios

Hibiscus is multicultural, specific to countries that get hot enough for them to flourish with their glorious flowers. In the Balkans the flowers are used to make tea, which is said to help lower cholesterol and lift the spirits. I love the idea that food can heal, repair and change things for the better – it's a nice way to live. How fulfilling to find a deeper meaning as to why certain recipes have been around for so many years.

The sour flavour of the hibiscus makes a lot of sense up against a pickle and it also dyes everything pink – what magic! You can most commonly find it in its dried version in Mediterranean or South-East Asian stores, which is what I've used in this recipe, but if you need to use tea bags because it's all you can find, no bother, just leave them in the pickling liquor for longer.

Make the pickling liquid in advance, if you can, to allow it time to chill, as the colder it is, the crunchier your pickles will be! You can halve this recipe if needs be but if you have the space, it's always good to get ahead on your pickling. You can omit the pistachios; I just like the texture.

The pickles will be ready to eat in three days and are sensational in a sandwich with lots of mayonnaise, some good ham and sharp Cheddar, or just about anything else you can put a pickle on.

MAKES 700G (1½LB)

1 litre (1¾ pints) white wine vinegar

500g (1lb 2oz) caster (superfine) sugar

Handful of dried hibiscus or 8 hibiscus tea bags

Juice of 2 lemons

2 large cucumbers

1 heaped tbsp salt

14 garlic cloves, thinly sliced

3 red onions, thinly sliced

150g (5½oz) pistachios, chopped, plus extra to garnish (optional)

Olive oil, for drizzling (optional)

Pour the vinegar and 200ml (7fl oz) water into a large saucepan over a medium heat. Add the sugar, dried hibiscus or tea bags and lemon juice. Bring to the boil, reduce the heat and simmer, stirring gently, for 10 minutes or until the sugar has dissolved. Remove from the heat and allow to cool completely before storing in the fridge until you are ready to pickle.

Slice the cucumbers into 1.5cm (½in) chunks and place in a large colander. Sprinkle over the salt, mix thoroughly, and allow to drain for a minimum of 3 hours and a maximum of 6.

Mix the cucumber, garlic, onion, and pistachios together until completely combined. Spoon the cucumber mixture into a sterilized jar (see page 21), pour over the pickling liquid and cover. The pickles will be ready to eat in 3 days and can be stored in the fridge for up to 6 months.

To serve as a side, top with the reserved pistachios and drizzle with olive oil.

Млечн

NOTINA

Dairy

An Ode
to Dairy

Self-sufficiency seems to be the buzzword of the moment. It's a concept that we've let slip through our fingers in favour of capitalism, losing further grip as borders and political tensions tighten and leave us all craving a slower, more natural way of living. It's a term that's less sought after in our region, as there is a strong sense of independence when it comes to agriculture and food in general in North Macedonia, a hangover from the days of Yugoslavian socialism.

There are many small-scale, family-run farms all over the country, as well as larger operations that deal with exports such as tobacco, fruits, vegetables, wheat and wine, and roughly 20 per cent of the population works in this sector (compared to 1 per cent in the UK). Aside from the exports, there's a common attitude, particularly among older generations, that they don't need much more than some homemade wines or spirits, a chunk of fresh bread and some cheeses. The small-scale farms exist to serve their own people, selling products at markets and ensuring the legacy of rural life is held on to and small batch production is celebrated and supported.

We know how to eat – a factory-produced block of yellow plastic-tasting Cheddar is just not going to cut it – and artisanal values have so long been commonplace in our kitchens. We have prized, native cheeses such as bieno sirenje (or "beaten cheese"), which is hard, bubbly and other-worldly salty, shaved like Parmesan and eaten on the side of any plate. When it comes to dairy farming, young white cheeses are the most common, with eggs or yufki (egg noodles) at breakfast, in salads, pastries, breads, with meat, on the barbecue or deep fried (as you'll notice as you work your way through the book). This chapter is a celebration of the cheesiest recipes you'll find in Balkan kitchens.

One family are taking the country by storm with their goat's milk products and their explosive enthusiasm for the rural way of life. I travelled to the village of Rashtak, a mere hour from the centre of Skopje and an area that has become known for small-scale farming. Leaving building blocks behind me, I approach the house to meet David and his parents, who had enough of the city and moved to Rashtak over a decade ago to pursue a life of farming and a preservation of traditions. The first thing he asks me is if

I've seen Pink Floyd in concert. I also notice a poster of The Doors over the barn as I take in my surroundings. No wonder he leans towards the sounds of progressive space-rock; the very vision of their home can carry you off into the fields like the lick on a psychedelic electric guitar.

The steps up to where they cook and sleep are guarded by a pregnant black cat and under the table is a bed full of newborn puppies. With little cages of maturing cheeses hung all around us, this tangible, open way of living washes over me; I'm going to really like it here. Besides feeling like I'm just about ready to deep dive into a life of farming, we begin to bond over our love for physical labour, eating, and the pure satisfaction that comes from both. David's parents have tried their hand at it all: growing mushrooms in their basement back in the city, running a kebab shop, a burekdzilnica (bakery), and a corner shop that sold all sorts. This was all to build a life for David and his sister, an energy I can feel pouring out of them as they revel in how hard they all work.

Their parenting worked – following a democratic vote at home one day, they all decided to move out to the village with David's grandparents, who needed the fresh air, and all of them seeking to put their ancestral land to good use finally. They feel a great responsibility to their ancestors, who had nothing, worked themselves to the bone and gave them what they can now enjoy today.

They had never kept goats before but decided to try, for their long lactation periods and abundant reproduction. A smart move indeed but at the time, goat milk was considered at the bottom of the dairy ladder, a perception that they have single-handedly changed. With no prior knowledge of livestock, breeding, or the production of cheeses, they learned everything in the first couple of years from literature, YouTube videos and, of course, the locals, armed only with a milk machine and their own fields of fertility. They are now known as the authority on all things goat-related. The flag of their business, Kozi Mleko Planina, meaning "goat, milk, mountain", waves in the wind behind us. Three words, one story, as David puts it. Happy goats, mild milk, and a seriously generous mountain means that they sell out of their small-production, high-quality cheeses very quickly.

David packs the boot of his dad's car with a giant cooler, blankets, and bottles. He tells me we are off for some fresh air, totally under-

selling the grandeur of the afternoon. We climb up to a clearing, David asking his dad to keep going further until we find the perfect spot under the shade of some trees, with the whole city beneath us like an emptied-out pool; a stark but beautiful contrast to all that surrounds us. He then lays out a picnic, designed to showcase his hustle, the deep love he has found in his art, and the awakening he has discovered through farming. We share an 18-month-old goat's cheese, drizzled with homemade saffron and truffle honey; soured goat's milk cream with herbs picked from the bushes next to us; a ricotta-style cheese smothered in his mum's thick, blackberry jam. I close my eyes and slip into the twilight zone, time screeching to a halt as I take considered bites and deep breaths, appreciating this exhibition of pure devotion to ancient skill.

Everything feels so familiar and everyone so much more open to a profound connection; we aren't just great hosts with our platters, we know how to make you feel welcome. We wrap up the day with a goat and kid meet and greet and I start to feel the heaviness of having to let this snapshot of rural existence go. I'll leave and he will go back to living life as if it's a miracle, embracing the connection between animal, land, sky, and the final product, walking the very same paths as his ancestors. David says his old, urban life is but a blur to him, almost as if it never happened, and I wonder how much easier one-dimensional experiences are to forget and how my journey through life in Rashtak will stay with me for the rest of time.

Fresh White Cheese

My previous life as a cheesemonger taught me that there is serious value in keeping the animals happy and in feeding them well, and how you can taste the fresh lavender in an earthy, young goat's cheese, and all the other elements from the fields. Use the best-quality milk you can find and make this in spring, then fall in love with this new, invaluable skill and go on a little cheese journey of your very own.

You can flavour the brine with fresh herbs, spices, or garlic. It's best eaten within seven days but bear in mind the taste and consistency will change over time.

SERVES 4

1 litre (1¾ pints) full-fat (whole) or
　Jersey milk

1 tbsp salt

1 tbsp rennet

Pour the milk into a large lidded saucepan and heat to just above body temperature – about 37°C (99°F). Remove from the heat and stir in the salt and rennet.

Put the lid on the pan and tightly wrap 2 blankets around it. Set aside for 5 hours.

Unwrap the pan and check that the cheese has set – it should appear as a solid circle in the middle of the pan with clear-ish liquid around it.

Line a fine mesh sieve with muslin (cheesecloth). Transfer the cheese to the sieve, wrap it up tightly in the muslin, and place a heavy bowl on top to press down on it . Place the sieve over a bowl and refrigerate for 10 hours, or overnight.

Carefully remove the cheese from the muslin. Store in an airtight container in the fridge and eat within 7 days. Delicious on its own or as part of a cheese board, or breaded and fried (see page 55).

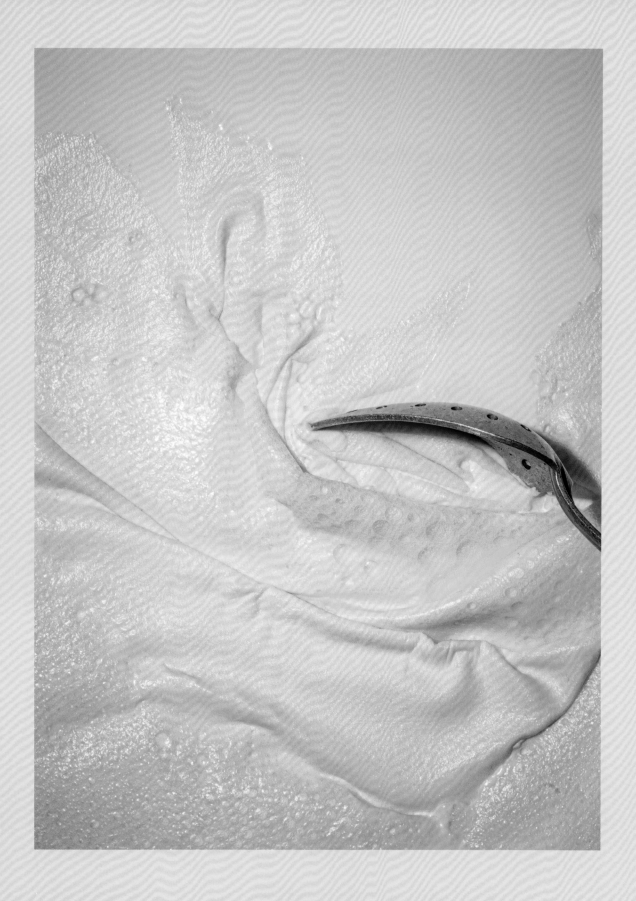

Kajmak

Ah, my beloved kajmak (pronounced "kaymak"), a precious and heavenly substance whose popularity stretches to Central Asia, the Levant, Turkey, Iran, and Iraq. Similar to a salted clotted cream, it's prized across the Balkans as the best butter is in France. There are a few ways to make it and they all require skill, loving care, and a whole lot of patience. Knowing how lengthy the process is, I can't quite fathom the impressive, giant wooden barrels (or cabrica) full of the stuff, you see huddled in the windows of dairy shops.

This recipe is for the young version, but it can also be fermented in the same barrels, resulting in a bright yellow, funky cream spread. Traditionally this should always be made with raw milk, but adding double (heavy) cream to pasteurized milk will do the trick.

Used in the Rebra U Kajmak on page 185, kajmak can be used just like butter or dolloped onto any form of grilled meat.

MAKES 500ML (16FL OZ)

1 litre (1¾ pints) full-fat (whole) milk
300ml (10fl oz) double (heavy) cream
Salt

Pour the milk and cream into a large, wide saucepan that's as clean as possible, and stir to combine. Place the pan over the lowest heat until you just begin to see bubbles appearing. Immediately remove from the heat and allow to cool for 2 hours or until a skin has formed on the surface.

Very carefully remove the skin from the surface of the milk using a slotted spoon and transfer the skin to a separate container. The spoon will help to drain off any excess milk but if you end up with a lot of milk in the container with the skin, drain it once again and return the milk to the pan.

Place the container in the fridge, then repeat the process of heating the milk and removing the skin on top, adding it to the container in the fridge, four times or until the fat content of the milk has reduced.

Using a fork, thoroughly mix the skins with a little salt. Blend or whip until smooth, if liked (I prefer it with a little more texture). It's at its best for 3 days, and can be kept in the fridge for up to 5.

Urda

I first made this whey cheese (pronounced "oorda") with my Uncle Kole and my Aunt Suze, who bought all the milk from the farm down the road from their home – gallons of raw, thick, almost cream-like milk. We spent a whole day analysing the curds, playing with temperatures and rennet, waiting on it all to strain and set, just in time for supper when we could gobble it all up. We made urda using kiselo mleko, which translates to "sour milk" but is closest to fermented yogurt, and I was blown away by this sour, ricotta-like young cheese and the simplicity of making it.

MAKES 600G (1LB 5OZ)

1 litre (1¾ pints) full-fat (whole) or Jersey milk
6 tbsp white wine vinegar
1 tbsp salt

Pour the milk, vinegar, and salt into a large saucepan over a medium heat and bring to the boil. Immediately reduce the heat to low and stir. You'll notice that the curds begin to float to the surface.

Heat for 30 minutes, stirring occasionally.

Line a fine mesh sieve with muslin (cheesecloth) and pour the curd and milk mixture into the sieve placed over a sink. Discard the milk.

Place the sieve containing the curds over a bowl and transfer to the fridge. Allow to drain for a couple of hours, then your cheese is ready! Eat within 5 days.

Urda is delicious served on toast and drizzled with honey. It can be used in Gibanica (see page 94) in place of the cottage cheese and is wonderful served with Slow Cooked Harissa Lamb (see page 166).

Nafora with Goat's Cheese, Candied Squash, and Caper Cream

Traditional Nafora is made by grilling chunks of bread and simply grating a tonne of white cheese on top and splashing over a good glug of oil – the perfect snack for drinking (usually ordered when the drinking has gone a little too far). Barbecue your bread if you can, but the grill (broiler) will also work just as well.

My version is inspired by David, the goats and his fields (see page 44). I was lucky enough to use his cheese and would highly recommend using local cheese from an independent supplier.

SERVES 6

150ml (5fl oz) vegetable or sunflower
  oil, plus extra for frying

1 bunch of mint, leaves picked

1 tbsp plain (all-purpose) flour

300g (10oz) unsliced white bread
  or white sourdough

Olive oil, for drizzling

200g (7oz) goat's cheese, crumbled

200g (7oz) Slatko – Tikva (see
  page 22)

Salt and freshly ground black pepper

For the caper cream

1 shallot, finely diced

200ml (7fl oz) double (heavy) cream

100g (3½oz) capers, finely chopped

Handful of parsley, finely chopped

1 tbsp Dijon mustard

To make the caper cream, heat a little oil in a frying pan over a medium heat. Add the shallot and cook, stirring, until softened. Slowly pour in the double cream. Gently whisk until thickened and reduced, about 2 minutes. Add the capers, parsley, mustard, and some seasoning, whisking for a further minute, then remove from the heat and set aside.

Heat the measured oil in a deep saucepan over a medium heat. Place the mint leaves into a bowl and season with a pinch of salt. Coat the leaves with the flour, taking care not to break them up. Drop 1 of the mint leaves into the oil to test if it is hot enough – if the leaf crisps, the oil is ready. Add the leaves to the oil and deep fry for 1–2 minutes, then drain on kitchen paper (paper towels).

Heat the grill (broiler) to high and cut the bread into 2.5cm (1in) chunks. Drizzle with the olive oil and grill until toasted, turning regularly.

Meanwhile reheat the caper cream over a low heat until warmed through.

To serve, drizzle a little of the caper cream onto a serving platter. Arrange the toasted bread, crumble over the goat's cheese, and scatter over the Slatko – Tikva. Drizzle with the remaining caper cream and top with the fried mint leaves.

Breaded White Cheese
with Urda and Apple Honey

I definitely don't shy away from the rapture found in over-indulgence, of double cheese and deep frying, of something sweet and sticky that's just the icing on the cake. Although nothing quite beats that first hot bite that makes you salivate uncontrollably, this is a perfect dish to be nibbled at, in honour of all the salty, fried cheeses that are laid out on kafana tables for hours, small chunks shared around the guests.

This is a very "loose" recipe because it's so versatile in terms of quantity, depending on the number of guests, or how strong the craving. Up the amounts of breadcrumbs/eggs/flour/cheese as you see fit.

MAKES 250ML (9FL OZ)

1 litre (1¾ pints) apple juice

300ml (10fl oz) vegetable oil, for frying

1 quantity Fresh White Cheese (see page 53)

100g (3½oz) panko breadcrumbs

2 eggs, whisked

100g (3½oz) plain (all-purpose) flour

1 quantity Urda (see page 52)

Salt and freshly ground black pepper

To make the apple honey, pour the apple juice into a large saucepan over a high heat. Bring to the boil, then reduce the heat to medium. Simmer for about 20 minutes, or until it has the consistency of runny honey. Remove from the heat and set aside to cool completely.

Heat the oil in a large saucepan over a medium heat for 8 minutes. Meanwhile, divide the cheese into 5 portions and pat dry using kitchen paper (paper towel). Place the breadcrumbs, eggs, and flour into separate shallow dishes and season each one well with salt and pepper.

Dip the white cheese portions in the flour first, followed by the egg and the breadcrumbs. Use one hand for the dry ingredients and the other for the egg, to avoid excess mess.

Carefully lower the cheese into the oil and fry for a minute or so on each side, or until golden brown – work in batches and don't overcrowd the pan to ensure the cheese is as crispy as possible. Drain the cheese on kitchen paper.

To serve, add a dollop of Urda to the crispy cheese and liberally drizzle with the apple honey.

Photographed on pages 56–57.

Pastrmalija with Taleggio, Burnt Butter, and Cold Tomato Sos

Pastrmajlijada is a festival held in the city of Stip, in North Macedonia. A whole community comes together to celebrate the pastrmalija (pronounced "pastrrmaliya"), which is similar to a crispy pizza, based on the Turkish pide. Although it's made across the country, Stip is where they do it like no other – a whole day of eating the best food the local restaurants and producers have to offer and drinking homemade wine. You don't need a ticket to attend, drinks aren't just served in cans, and I bet you don't have to wait hours in line for the toilet – definitely my kind of festival!

Pastrmalija is usually made with salted beef or pork and sometimes cheese, with a cracked egg added at the end and served with a pickled pepper. This is my rich version and, as per my favourite pizza restaurant in North Macedonia, 511, it's served with a cold sos (sauce) drizzled over to lift the abundance of cheese.

For a traditional take on this dish, marinate small cubes of pork in salt and pepper overnight and top the bread with it, cracking an egg over the top five minutes before it's finished cooking.

SERVES 4–8

For the dough

100ml (3½fl oz) milk

7g (¼oz) packet fast action yeast

1 tsp sugar

400g (14oz) plain (all-purpose) flour

1 egg

1 tsp salt

2 tbsp olive oil, plus extra for greasing

For the cold tomato sos

Vegetable or sunflower oil, for frying

6 garlic cloves, roughly chopped

400g (14oz) can chopped tomatoes

2 tbsp sugar

2 tsp dried oregano

1 tsp salt

For the toppings

100g (3½oz) butter

2 eggs, whisked

500g (1lb 2oz) Taleggio, well chilled

Salt

To make the dough, gently heat the milk until it's lukewarm to touch – be careful to not overheat it or it will kill the yeast. Combine the yeast, sugar, and 3 tbsp of the flour with the warm milk in a jug (measuring cup). Cover with a tea towel and set aside in a warm place for 10–15 minutes or until frothy.

Sift the remaining flour into a bowl and add the egg, salt, and oil. Gradually add the yeast mixture and about 100ml (3½fl oz) water at room temperature (you may not need all of the water). Bring the mixture together and lightly knead with your hands after each addition to form a smooth dough that doesn't stick to the bowl.

Turn the dough out onto a lightly floured work-surface and knead for 10 minutes. Transfer the dough into a large well-oiled bowl, cover with cling film (plastic wrap) and then a tea towel and set aside in a warm place for about an hour or until doubled in size.

To make the tomato sauce, heat a splash of oil in a frying pan over a low heat and add the garlic. Gently fry until softened, then add the remaining ingredients. Increase the heat to medium, bring to the boil, then reduce the heat to low and simmer for 15 minutes. Transfer to a food processor or blender and blend until smooth. Set aside to cool and then refrigerate until you're ready to serve.

Punch the dough down and divide it into 2 balls, then re-cover and leave to rise for a further 30 minutes.

To make the toppings, melt the butter in a frying pan over a medium heat for 10 minutes or until it's dark brown – this will give the dish its warming flavour. Set aside.

Preheat the oven to 200°C (180°C fan/400°F/Gas 6). Turn the dough out onto a lightly floured work-surface. Roll each dough ball into an oval shape, about 1cm (½in) thick. The outside of the oval should be a little thicker than the centre – if you're struggling to get the shape, just use your hands to pinch and pull on the outside a little. Fold the outside of the dough inwards to make a crust, ensuring it's as even as possible.

Set half of the burnt butter aside. Cover the centre of both dough ovals (not the crust) with the other half of the burnt butter and then carefully spread almost all of the whisked egg, seasoned with a pinch of salt, on top. Reserve a little of the egg to egg wash the crust to make it nice and shiny.

Slice the Taleggio straight from the fridge and spread out evenly on top of the egg. Brush the crust with the reserved egg and transfer the dough ovals to well-oiled baking trays. Bake in the oven for 20 minutes or until the middle of the dough is cooked and the crust is a deep golden brown.

Drizzle the remaining burnt butter over the pastrmalija and serve with the cold sos for dipping or drizzling.

Photographed on page 60.

Guinness Cheese Proja Melt

This denser, less sweet version of cornbread is most popular in Serbia, Bosnia, and North Macedonia. It started life in rural villages as an inexpensive and filling snack but its long-lasting popularity proves that it's so much more than that; I think proja may live forever.

In this base recipe I use cottage cheese as a nod to my parents who, in their first years in the UK, couldn't find anything that resembled their beloved white cheeses. I feel a little grip on my heart when I think of how many flavours they must have longed for. I wonder when they had their first pint of shandy, what pub it was in, did they buy a bag of pork scratchings or did they opt for dry roasted peanuts, will they ever feel as Balkan-British as me?

The base recipe for proja can be eaten for breakfast with eggs, as a side with stews or soups, or just as a premium snack.

MAKES 12 SLICES

For the proja

320g (11oz) plain full-fat yogurt

1 bunch of chives, thinly sliced

6 eggs

200ml (7fl oz) sunflower oil

300g (10oz) plain full-fat cottage cheese

200g (7oz) cornmeal

90g (3¼oz) plain (all-purpose) flour

1 heaped tsp baking powder

1 tsp salt

For the cheese sauce

35g (1¼oz) butter

1 tbsp English mustard

1 medium onion, finely diced

4 tbsp plain (all-purpose) flour

70ml (2¼fl oz) full-fat (whole) milk

70ml (2¼fl oz) Guinness

300g (10oz) grated Cheddar

300g (10oz) grated Gouda

240g (8½oz) grated mozzarella

Salt and freshly ground black pepper

Photographed on page 61.

Preheat the oven to 180°C (160°C fan/350°F/Gas 4). Grease a medium-large, deep baking pan (mine is 23 x 33cm/9 x 13in – bear in mind that the smaller the pan, the longer it will take to cook, and the larger it is, the thinner your bread will be and the quicker it will bake).

To make the proja, combine the yogurt with the chives and set aside. Whisk the eggs using an electric hand whisk (hand mixer) for 5 minutes or until fluffy (this stage is the key to a good proja, so don't rush it!).

Slowly add the oil the eggs, whisking continuously, then with the whisk still running add the yogurt and cottage cheese, followed by the flours, baking powder, and salt. Whisk for a further 5 minutes until the mixture is bubbly.

Pour the mixture into the prepared tin and bake for 30 minutes or until a knife inserted into the centre comes out clean. The proja can be baked in advance and finished with the topping just before serving, or you can stop here and enjoy the proja as it is.

To make the sauce, melt the butter and mustard in a medium non-stick saucepan over a low heat. Add the onion and fry until softened. Add the flour and cook for a further 3 minutes, whisking continuously, to form a roux.

Slowly add the milk, whisking after each addition, until the mixture is smooth and lump-free, then add the Guinness a little at a time, whisking continuously until thickened – this will take about 5 minutes.

Add the cheeses, a handful at a time, and mix until melted. Season and cook for a further 10 minutes or until thickened. Meanwhile, preheat the oven to 180°C (160°C fan/350°F/Gas 4) if necessary.

Pour the sauce all over the proja and return it to the oven for 10 minutes.

Allow to cool slightly before slicing and serving. Store any leftovers in the fridge for up to 4 days. The proja also freezes really well.

Mekici with Gorgonzola Sauce and Roasted Grapes

When a new, little life is brought into the world, mekici (meaning "softness" and pronounced "mekitsi") are traditionally made to welcome them. Piles of fried dough are torn by many joyful hands and are either made at home or pre-ordered from bakeries and restaurants. The bus that takes you from Skopje to Ohrid makes a pit-stop at a large, unassuming café with the usual road fuel of snacks, pastries, and coffee, but there is also a little hatch that opens up when someone orders the mekici. A master is revealed, and a woman sends out freshly fried works of art, known country-wide for being the best, huge, pillowy, warm, greasy wonders that you can take back on the bus in a paper bag with a big chunk of cheese. Mekici are also eaten for breakfast and the most classic combination is brined white cheese and a sweet jam; try that first and then give my version a go.

The mekici are best eaten the day they are made but if you have any leftovers, just reheat them on a tray in the oven or in a toastie maker. You can use any blue cheese for the sauce but for me, nothing beats the creaminess of gorgonzola dolce.

MAKES 8

For the roasted grapes

500g (1lb 2oz) grapes
1 tbsp sugar
1 tbsp white wine vinegar
Olive oil, for drizzling
Salt and freshly ground black pepper

For the mekici

7g (¼oz) packet fast action yeast
1 tsp caster (superfine) sugar
1 tsp baking powder
400g (14oz) plain (all-purpose) flour
200g (7oz) full-fat plain yogurt
1 egg
About 400ml (14fl oz) vegetable or
  sunflower oil, for frying and oiling

For the gorgonzola sauce

Vegetable or sunflower oil, for frying
2 shallots, finely chopped
2 garlic cloves, finely chopped
300ml (10fl oz) double (heavy) cream
200g (7oz) gorgonzola dolce
Salt and freshly ground black pepper

To make the roasted grapes, preheat the oven to 220°C (200°C fan/425°F/Gas 7). Place the grapes into a bowl with the sugar, vinegar, seasoning, and a drizzle of olive oil. Stir gently to coat the grapes.

Transfer the grapes to a baking tray and roast in the oven for 10–12 minutes or until the grapes start to burst. Remove from the oven, allow to cool and stir before serving.

To make the mekici, combine the yeast, sugar, and 80ml (2¾fl oz) lukewarm water in a jug (measuring cup). Cover with a tea towel and set aside in a warm place for 10–15 minutes or until frothy. Meanwhile mix the baking powder into the flour and set aside.

Pour the yeast mixture into a bowl and add the yogurt and egg. Mix well. Gradually add the flour and bring the mixture together with your hands, scraping any excess from the sides as you go, to form a sticky dough. Turn the dough out onto a very lightly floured worksurface and knead for about 10 minutes (the dough needs to remain sticky, so use as little flour as possible).

Transfer the dough to a well-oiled bowl, cover with a tea towel and leave in a warm place to rise for about 90 minutes.

Pour a little oil into a bowl for oiling your hands, then heat the remaining oil in a large, wide saucepan over a medium-low heat for 8 minutes.

When the oil is ready, grab a handful of the dough and stretch it into a circle about 1cm (½in) thick. I find that holding the dough at the edges and letting it pull out naturally works best, working my way around. If it's easier, you can divide the dough into 8 balls before you start frying and shape them as you go.

Gently lower the mekici into the oil and as soon as they start to float, carefully spoon some oil over the top so that they cook evenly. Cook for 1 minute on each side or until puffed-up and golden brown but not crispy.

Remove the mekici using a slotted spoon and drain on kitchen paper (paper towel). Repeat with the remaining dough.

The mekici are best eaten as quickly as possible but if you want to make them ahead of time, they can be reheated in the oven the following day.

To make the sauce, heat a splash of oil in a medium frying pan over a low heat. Add the shallots and fry for 5 minutes, stirring constantly, or until completely softened. Add the garlic and continue to cook for 1 minute.

Pour the cream into the pan and crumble over the cheese. Stir until the cheese has completely melted, then continue to cook, stirring occasionally, for about 15 minutes or until the sauce has reduced. Season and serve the mekici topped with the sauce and roasted grapes.

Photographed on pages 66–67.

Tec

Baking

At Home with Natasa

The power of flour is meaningful; an important current that runs through centuries and cultures. It must have been written about a trillion times in countless cookbooks because flour belongs to all of us. If we have been given the gift of not only life but of wheat, the means to form it into a whole universe of ways, to fill us up and to enjoy it in all its million forms, even when pushed to the brink, we should count ourselves lucky.

I've always been told that flour is just different in the Balkans. My younger eyes were not sharp enough to notice but as I sat across from Natasa and watched as it fell through her fingers, my pupils widened at how soft and super fine it was, pure as a pile of pearls.

We were at her home in the small, hillside village of Ramne, just above Lake Ohrid, after Natasa picked me up from my Aunt Mare and Uncle Rade's. They insisted on meeting her, slowly coming all the way down to the gate to make sure they made a connection by finding out more about her family; a typical sign of a close-knit society and a gracious need to formally welcome someone into the fold. They had been asking me all morning, in as many different ways as possible, if she was the woman they saw cooking on TV,

a fact she later confirms, satisfying them with her warmth and receptiveness of their interest in all that she does.

On the steep drive to her home I learned about Natasa's difficult childhood; her father passed away at a young age and her mum had to sustain her and her sister while also taking care of her elderly parents. Her mother was a hero to her, and she wanted to help and to be more like her. So as a child she started a notebook, observing her mum while she cooked, secretly taking notes, determined to relieve her in the kitchen. Women in North Macedonia have long been revered as guardians of tradition. Her face lit up as she talked about her family, including the men, hard workers with a deep appreciation for food. Both Natasa and her sister started baking early on, when they would be given a piece of dough each to create something with, a practice that instilled pride in them. They would relish in and savour every bite of the beauty that they had created themselves.

Natasa's words seem to drift through the fresh herbs and vegetable garden, float up above her farm, and fall over the lake below us. I feel so comfortable listening to her speak, both of us holding giant tears in the corners of eyes as we connect over the desire to honour those before us, all the skilful hands that raised us, the love that has always surrounded and swallowed us up, like the meals we always had in front of us as children.

After a welcoming bite of her watermelon slatko (see page 24) she lights the wood fire oven and prepares the stand, the pirustija which she will bake the pies on, under the sach – a metal cloche that essentially holds in the heat from the fire. A feast, a whole catalogue of ancient recipes that make the most of her beloved dough. I follow her as she collects the eggs from the chicken hatch and chard from the vegetable patch, and it dawns on me that this is probably going to be one of the best meals I've ever eaten.

As she starts to prepare a selection of pastries, the speed at which she works and the strength of her hands hypnotizes me, so graceful and powerful at the same time. They say you shouldn't bake when you're upset, but from experience this is a good time to knead, roll, stretch, and fold.

Before Natasa married the love of her life, Vasko, she didn't have a connection with the countryside but Ramne became and will always be her place of soul searching, and she adored it enough to raise her children there. Little by little they worked on the house, planting fruits and vegetables and keeping animals, even cows so that she can make cheese for her pastries. As the home came together, they started to have family and friends over, cooking the most traditional of recipes, sparking an idea to share this way of living with others, as a form of authentic, rural tourism.

Pirustija Nedanoski, the name of Natasa's house and business, was born out of a burning desire to return to nature and to find new strength and meaning from the village; and anyone can book a stay to do just that. Guests can get involved with the baking process, learning techniques that are so old they're not commonplace. Natasa makes a good point that it's all well and good preserving traditions but it's probably more important to pass them on, most notably to younger generations.

All of this unravels from within her as she's stood by the intensity of the fire, checking on the crackling pies, puffing up; she's covered in sweat, talking about the satisfaction she gets from surrounding herself with people that are interested in traditions and that value hard work. She's spiritually nourished by her very own authenticity and a commitment to reach new levels of historical depth.

Dinner is hot crunchy pies, heaving tomatoes, jars of preserves and a bottle of sweet red wine. Natasa whips off her dusty apron and takes a sip, wipes her brow, and I think about what she said earlier, how all of this just makes her a better person. As I sweep my plate with a burnt crust, soaking up the juice from the tomatoes, scooping on a dollop of cheese, I sit back and think: you've always been this way, you just needed to find your way back home, and that's something my new friend and I will always have in common.

Koshmis Pita with Cheese

This cheese pie would have been traditionally cooked under a sach – a large metal pot placed over the pie and covered with hot coals. You may not get the flavour of the fire, but the oven works perfectly well. You can swap out the filling for meat, spinach, Swiss chard, a cheese of your choice; the possibilities are endless. This really works best, as with any dough, made in a warm kitchen on a warm day.

SERVES 12

150ml (5fl oz) milk

7g (¼oz) packet fast action yeast

½ tsp sugar

3 eggs

400g (14oz) brined white cheese
   or feta, crumbled

500g (1lb 2oz) plain (all-purpose)
   flour, sifted

1 tsp salt

Oil, for oiling the bowl

150g (5½oz) butter, melted

5 tbsp cornflour (cornstarch)

Gently heat the milk until it's lukewarm to touch – be careful to not overheat it or it will kill the yeast.

Combine the yeast, sugar, and warm milk in a jug (measuring cup). Cover with a tea towel and set aside in a warm place for 10–15 minutes or until frothy. Meanwhile, mix the eggs and cheese together in a bowl until combined and set aside.

Pour the yeast mixture into a bowl and slowly incorporate the flour and salt using your hands.

Add about 150ml (5fl oz) warm water, a little at a time, lightly kneading between additions to form a dough. You may need more or less water, depending on the temperature of your kitchen. The dough should be sticky but easy to handle.

Turn the dough out onto a lightly floured work-surface and knead for 10 minutes. Transfer the dough into a large well-oiled bowl, cover with cling film (plastic wrap) and then a tea towel, and set aside in a warm place for about an hour or until doubled in size.

Turn the dough out onto the worksurface once more and knead for a further 10 minutes. Divide into 6 balls and then divide each ball into 3.

Roll each ball into a 1cm (½in) circle. Brush half of the melted butter over the circles and sprinkle generously with cornflour. Stack 3 circles on top of each other and repeat for the remaining circles until you have 6 piles. Cover with a tea towel and set aside to rise for 30 minutes.

Butter a 30cm (12in) round baking dish and preheat the oven to 200°C (180°C fan/400°F/Gas 6). Roll each pastry stack into a larger circle to fit inside the baking dish. Brush a circle with some of the remaining butter and place into the baking dish. Spread with some of the cheese and egg mixture, then stack another buttered pastry circle on top. Repeat to create 5 layers.

Add the final pastry circle, brush with the last of the butter, and cut into squares, slicing each square in the middle to allow the pastry to puff up.

Bake in the oven for 30–35 minutes, or until golden brown. Enjoy this gift from my ancestors.

Pogacha

This hearty white bread would have been traditionally baked on the hearth using embers from the fire. Always served at Christmas, New Year, and Easter, it's also made to mark Saints' Day on the Orthodox calendar. Mum would lower the impressive dough crown of glory to top off the heaving buffet table, and serve it to scoop up her sausage casserole, made with the best British bangers she could find.

SERVES 10

250ml (9fl oz) milk

7g (¼oz) packet fast action yeast

1 tsp caster (superfine) sugar

4 eggs plus 3 yolks

(1¼ tbsp) vegetable oil, plus extra to oil the bowl

700g (1½lb) plain (all-purpose) flour, sifted

2 tsp salt

200g (7oz) brined white cheese or feta, crumbled

150g (5½oz) butter, melted

Sesame seeds, for sprinkling

Gently heat the milk until it's lukewarm to touch – be careful to not overheat it or it will kill the yeast. Combine the yeast, sugar, and warm milk in a jug (measuring cup). Cover with a tea towel and set aside in a warm place for 10–15 minutes or until frothy.

Pour the yeast mixture into a clean bowl. Add 2 of the whole eggs and gradually incorporate the oil, flour, and salt, using your hands to form a smooth dough.

Turn the dough out onto a lightly floured worksurface and knead for 10 minutes. Transfer to a well-oiled bowl, cover with cling film (plastic wrap) and a tea towel and place in a warm place for about an hour or until doubled in size.

Turn the dough out onto the worksurface and knead for a further 10 minutes. Set aside.

Preheat the oven to 180°C (160°C fan/350°F/Gas 4). Mix the remaining 2 whole eggs and the cheese together in a bowl until thoroughly combined and set aside.

Divide the dough into 3 balls. Roll each ball into a 3mm (⅛in) thick rectangle. Spread a thick layer of melted butter over each dough rectangle, followed by the cheese and egg mixture, spreading evenly and leaving 2cm (¾in) of the dough uncovered at the edges.

Roll-up each dough rectangle widthways as neatly as possible and then cut triangles along the roll about 5cm (2in) thick at the widest part. Arrange the rolls on a well-oiled 25 x 25cm (10 x 10in) baking tray, starting on the outside and working your way in.

Cover the tray with a tea towel and set aside to rise for 15 minutes. Meanwhile, whisk the 3 egg yolks.

Brush the egg yolk all over the pogacha. Sprinkle with sesame seeds and bake in the oven for 30–40 minutes or until deep golden brown.

Kifli

Somewhere between a fancy hotel dinner roll and a croissant, kifli are a vital part of Balkan baking. The union of butter and sesame drifting out of the gaps in the oven gives me the same olfactory memory as my best friend's mum, Bhapinder, toasting her infamous chapatis, or the warmth coming from the tortilla factory near my house in Brooklyn. It's precious how these familiar smells can spark so much affection, no matter the cuisine.

MAKES 12 ROLLS

100ml (3½fl oz) full-fat (whole) milk

7g (¼oz) packet fast action yeast

½ tsp caster (superfine) sugar

450g (1lb) plain (all-purpose) flour, sifted

1 tbsp salt

1 tsp baking powder

100ml (3½fl oz) full-fat plain yogurt

3 eggs plus 2 yolks

90g (3¼oz) butter at room temperature

Sesame seeds, for sprinkling

Sea salt, for sprinkling

Gently heat the milk until it's lukewarm to touch – be careful to not overheat it or it will kill the yeast. Combine the yeast, sugar, and warm milk in a jug (measuring cup). Cover with a tea towel and set aside in a warm place for 10–15 minutes or until frothy.

Combine the flour, salt and baking powder in a bowl and pour over the yeast mixture. Stir to incorporate the wet ingredients into the dry. Gradually add the yogurt, 1 of the whole eggs and 200ml (7fl oz) lukewarm water and bring the dough together with your hands.

Turn the dough out onto a lightly floured worksurface and knead for 10 minutes. Transfer to a well-oiled bowl, cover with cling film (plastic wrap) and a tea towel and place in a warm place for about an hour or until doubled in size.

Turn the dough out onto the worksurface once more and knead for a further 10 minutes. Set aside.

Preheat the oven to 180°C (160°C fan/350°F/Gas 4). Place a deep baking tray in the bottom of the oven and half fill with hot water; this will create steam and perfect the texture of the bread.

Divide the dough in 2 and roll each half into a circle measuring around 28cm (11in). Mix 40g (1½oz) of the butter with the remaining 2 whole eggs and brush this all over each dough circle.

Cut each circle into 6 even triangles and add a dollop of the remaining butter to the centre of each triangle.

Carefully roll each triangle from the outside of the circle towards the centre to make a shape similar to a croissant. Ensure they are as tightly rolled as possible – they tend to try to pop open when they bake, so use a little extra egg to seal if needed.

Transfer the kifli onto a well-oiled baking sheet and brush with the egg yolks, then sprinkle with the sesame seeds and sea salt. Bake for 20 minutes or until golden brown.

Lepinja

I won't spark a debate as to who made these first, but whoever it was and wherever they may have been: thank you. These chewy, distinctive breads are crucial to barbecue restaurants; finished off on the grill until fluffy, there's no better doughy accompaniment for all the punchy juices, as you'll find out once you try the Kebapcinja on page 164. The very idea of them evokes memories of trolleys, piled high with the bouncing breads, chattering across the cobbled stones of the Old Bazaar in Skopje (photographed), making their way to the countless grill restaurants to be served up with raw onion, Kajmak (see page 51), maybe a whole hot pepper, and a platter of barbecued meats.

These breads are traditionally baked using stone; a pizza oven works well. A tasty alternative is frying them gently and drizzling with lashings of good olive oil.

MAKES 6

3 tbsp milk

7g (¼oz) packet fast action yeast

1 tsp caster (superfine) sugar

1 tsp salt

About 400g (14oz) plain (all-purpose) flour, sifted

240ml (8fl oz) sparkling water

Gently heat the milk until it's lukewarm to touch – be careful to not overheat it or it will kill the yeast. Combine the yeast, sugar, and warm milk in a jug. Cover with a tea towel and set aside in a warm place for 10–15 minutes or until frothy. Meanwhile, stir the salt into the flour and set aside.

Pour the yeast mixture into a large bowl with the sparkling water (make sure that it's as fizzy and fresh as possible). Gradually add the flour and bring the mixture together with your hands, scraping any excess from the sides as you go, to form a slightly sticky dough. You may need a little more or less flour depending on the temperature of your kitchen.

Turn the dough out onto a very lightly floured worksurface and knead for about 10 minutes (the dough needs to remain sticky, so use as little flour as possible) or until the dough is silky smooth and bouncy. Transfer to a well-oiled bowl, cover with a couple of tea towels and leave in a warm place for 90 minutes or until doubled in size.

Punch the dough down, re-cover and leave to rise for a further hour.

Punch the dough down again and divide into 6 evenly sized balls. Set aside to rest on a baking tray for 15 minutes.

Gently roll each ball out until about 1cm (½in) thick (to keep as much air in as possible I use my hands to gently shape the dough rather than a rolling pin) then arrange them onto a lined or floured baking sheet. Cover with a tea towel and set aside to rise for a further 20 minutes.

Preheat the oven to 220°C (200°C fan/425°F/Gas 7). Place a deep baking tray in the bottom of the oven and half fill with hot water; this will create steam and perfect the texture of the breads.

Bake the breads for 5 minutes, then reduce the heat to 160°C (140°C fan/325°F/Gas 3) and bake for a further 10–12 minutes until golden brown in colour and puffed-up.

Remove from the oven and cover with a clean, damp tea towel for 10 minutes to soften the crust.

Rhubarb and Poppy Seed Buns

The opium poppy is the national flower of North Macedonia; you'll find them on the coat of arms and growing in dense bundles of rapture throughout the spring months.

Many people believe in the health benefits of poppy seeds and eat them straight from the jar to keep a spring in their step. There's even a family business in Skopje called BioOil MK that produces collagen and oils by cold pressing the superstar seed, hoping to help people with an array of ailments. In the Balkans and in many areas of Eastern Europe, opium poppy seeds are used in recipes for roulade and strudel; sweet layers of crunchy, soft, dense, nutty, and bitter-sweet deliciousness all rolled up in doughy bread. The rhubarb in this version cuts through the bitterness of the seeds and is at its best in spring. Using forced rhubarb when it's in season will make sure your syrup is super pink, but if you're using regular rhubarb you can add a drop of pink food colouring if you like.

SERVES 10

For the buns
230ml (7¾fl oz) milk

7g (¼oz) packet fast action yeast

50g (1¾oz) caster (superfine) sugar

½ tsp salt

2 tbsp vegetable oil

1 egg

90g (3¼oz) butter at room temperature, plus extra for greasing

About 550g (1¼lb) plain (all-purpose) flour, sifted

200ml (7fl oz) soured cream, to serve

For the filling
350–400g (12–14oz) rhubarb, roughly chopped

Zest and juice of 1 lemon

250g (9oz) caster (superfine) sugar

35g (1¼oz) toasted poppy seeds

For the syrup
250g (9oz) caster (superfine) sugar

Handful of dried hibiscus or 1 hibiscus tea bag

To make the filling, add the rhubarb, 50ml (1¾fl oz) water, lemon zest and juice, and sugar to a medium saucepan over a high heat and bring to the boil. Reduce the heat to medium and cook for 20–30 minutes or until the mixture resembles jam. Remove 2 tbsp of the filling and set aside. Add the poppy seeds to the pan, stir, and set aside to cool.

To make the buns, gently heat the milk until it's lukewarm to touch – be careful to not overheat it or it will kill the yeast.

Combine the yeast, a pinch of the sugar, and the warm milk in a jug (measuring cup). Cover with a tea towel and set aside in a warm place for 10–15 minutes or until frothy.

Meanwhile combine the remaining sugar, salt, oil, egg, and butter in a bowl.

Pour the yeast mixture into the bowl. Gradually add the flour and bring the mixture together with your hands, scraping any excess from the sides as you go, to form a smooth and slightly sticky dough. You may need a little more or less flour depending on the temperature of your kitchen.

Turn the dough out onto a lightly floured surface and knead for 10 minutes. Cover with cling film (plastic wrap) and a tea towel and leave in a warm place for about an hour or until doubled in size.

Preheat the oven to 180°C (160°C fan/350°F/Gas 4). Turn the dough out onto the worksurface once more and knead for a further 10 minutes. Divide the dough in 2 and roll each half into a rectangle about 1cm (½in) thick.

Evenly spread half of the rhubarb and poppy seed filling onto each rectangle and then roll the rectangles up tightly lengthways. Cut each roll into 12 equal portions.

Arrange the rolls in a greased 25cm (10in) round cake tin so that the spirals are facing up, then cover with a tea towel and leave to rise for 15 minutes. Bake in the oven for 25–30 minutes.

Meanwhile, make the syrup. Place the reserved 2 tbsp of rhubarb filling into a small saucepan over a medium heat. Add 100ml (3½fl oz) water, the sugar, and hibiscus. Stir to combine and bring to the boil. Boil for about 5 minutes (don't be tempted to stir!) or until a syrup forms. Pass the syrup through a sieve and set aside.

Brush the syrup all over the tops of the buns as soon as they come out of the oven to add an all-important flush of pink, retaining a little to swirl through the soured cream. Serve the buns with a big dollop of soured cream, drizzled with the remaining syrup, in the centre for dipping.

Photographed on pages 86-87.

Burek

I won't give you all the keys to my pastry castle but by using shop-bought filo (phyllo) pastry, you'll be armed with the ingredient to make a savoury pie that comes pretty damn close to Macedonian burek (pronounced "boorek"). If you have a Mediterranean or Middle Eastern shop near you then try out a bottle of Aryan drinking yogurt with this, taking sips between every bite, or just revel in the beauty of burek any time of day.

You can swap out the minced meat for pretty much any filling you fancy; just avoid anything that's too wet or the pastry will become soggy. I use a 23cm (9in) round cake tin for my burek but you can use any size or shape you have to hand; just bear in mind that the thinner the tin, the less cooking the burek will need.

SERVES 4

200ml (7fl oz) vegetable oil, plus extra for frying and greasing

1 onion, finely chopped

500g (1lb 2oz) beef mince (ground beef), at least 20% fat

2 garlic cloves, finely chopped

2 tsp salt

Cracked black pepper, to taste

4 eggs

500g (1lb 2oz) filo (phyllo) pastry

Sparkling water, for sprinkling

Preheat the oven to 180°C (160°C fan/350°F/Gas 4). To make the filling, heat a little oil in a frying pan over a medium heat and cook the onion for 5 minutes or until soft. Add the beef, garlic, and 1 tsp of the salt and break up the meat so there are no large clumps. Cook for about 5 minutes or until the beef is browned and cooked through. Season with black pepper and set aside to cool. You don't want the mince to dry out too much, as the fat is going to be super delicious when it sinks into the pastry.

Whisk the eggs and measured oil together with the remaining teaspoon of salt. Remove the filo from the packaging and lay onto a chopping board or clean worksurface. Cover with a damp tea towel so it doesn't dry out too much.

Lay a sheet of filo into a well-oiled 30cm (12in) round cake tin – any filo that doesn't fit in the tin can be scrunched-up around the edges to form a crust. Brush with some of the egg and oil mixture. Repeat with a further 3 filo sheets to create the base for the pie.

Spoon some of the filling into the tin and spread it evenly over the pastry. Carefully scrunch up 2 sheets of pastry a little to create layers and arrange in the tin. Brush the pastry with the egg and oil mixture and sprinkle with a little sparkling water. Repeat until you have 4 sheets of pastry left.

Layer the final 4 sheets of pasty into the tin, brushing each with the egg and oil mixture, to create a crust.

Bake in the oven for 25–30 minutes or until deep, golden brown. Allow to cool for 15 minutes before slicing. Burek freezes really well – just defrost and reheat in the oven before serving.

Hot Fried Cheese Burek Loaf
with Chilli and Honey

This version of burek takes a different shape to the one on page 88 as it's baked in a tin loaf tin. Many things taste better once fried, but there's something other-worldly about fried pastry. The slices of this loaf should be almost burnt in the pan and outrageously crunchy in contrast to the soft, pillowy layers in the middle. It's great on its own, but even better served in a gorgeous pool of oil and honey. I used a 900g (2lb) loaf tin. You can use any size loaf tin, just bear in mind that you may have to adjust the bake time – the deeper the tin, the longer it will take to bake.

SERVES 6

500g (1lb 2oz) filo (phyllo) pastry

2 garlic cloves, finely chopped

200ml (7fl oz) runny honey

3 eggs

100ml (3½fl oz) vegetable oil, plus extra for greasing and frying

250g (9oz) feta, crumbled, or cheese of your choice

Preserved Lemon and Garlic Crispy Chilli Oil (see page 37), strained if liked, or store-bought chilli oil, to taste

Salt and freshly ground black pepper

Remove the filo pastry from the fridge 15 minutes before you wish to use it and set aside. Preheat the oven to 180°C (160°C fan/350°F/Gas 4). Combine the garlic and honey in a bowl and set aside (this can be done the day before so it has more time to infuse).

Remove the filo pastry from its packet and cover with a damp tea towel to stop it from drying out. Whisk 2 of the eggs with the oil and season to taste.

Grease a 900g (2lb) loaf tin with oil. Arrange a sheet of filo in the tin, layering and scrunching the pastry to fit, then brush all over with the egg wash. Repeat to create 4 layers.

Crumble some feta over the pastry, then scrunch up 2 sheets of pastry and layer over the feta. Brush the pastry with the egg wash and repeat until all the feta has been used, reserving 3 sheets of pastry for the top.

Lay the first of the reserved pastry sheets over the loaf and brush with the egg wash. Repeat with the remaining 2 reserved sheets. Fold in any excess pastry – this will form a delicious crust.

Whisk the remaining egg and use it to brush the top of the loaf. Bake for 25 minutes or until the top of the loaf is a deep golden brown. Remove the loaf from the oven and allow to cool completely in the tin before slicing.

Pour the garlic-infused honey into a small saucepan over a low heat and warm until slightly thinned, then strain using a fine-meshed sieve or muslin cloth (cheesecloth) to remove the garlic.

To serve, heat a little oil in a frying pan over a high heat. Slice the cooled loaf into 4cm (1½in) slices and fry the slices for 2–3 minutes on each side or until crispy and beginning to char. Drizzle the burek slices with chilli oil and garlic honey and serve.

Gibanica

Gibanica (pronounced "geebanitsa") is an egg and cheese pie with a fluffy, soft middle and a crunchy, flaky filo (phyllo) pastry exterior. Gibanica is where it all began for me: my nan's infamous pie that kicked off an entirely new life and business and the recipe I am most grateful to have been gifted. I'm not sure if I'll ever be able to recreate what her hands were able to do, as like most Balkan grandmas and aunties, recipes aren't always what they seem, and once you start following their scribbles you realize they're just guides – nothing is exact and measurements are personal, just as personal as the recipes themselves. While writing this book it's been a real challenge to decipher them and although it's left me pulling my hair out at times, it's also made me giggle – was the plan all along to ensure that no one could ever make it quite the same? A dear family friend, Slavica, surprised me recently with the information that once her gibanica is baked, she carefully balances it on upturned glasses to ensure the bottom stays crispy; a crucial detail in perfecting her pie but, funnily enough, left out of the recipe she passed down to me.

I use a 25cm (10in) round cake tin for my gibanica but you can use any size or shape you have to hand, just bear in mind that the thinner you go, the less cooking it will need.

Photographed on pages 96–97.

SERVES 8

8 eggs
300g (10oz) plain cottage cheese
1 tbsp salt, plus extra for seasoning
120ml (4fl oz) vegetable oil, plus extra for oiling
200g (7oz) feta, crumbled
500g (1lb 2oz) filo (phyllo) pastry
Sparkling water, for sprinkling

Preheat the oven to 180°C (160°C fan/350°F/Gas 4). Whisk 6 of the eggs in a large bowl until fluffy. Add the cottage cheese, salt, 70ml (2¼fl oz) of the oil and the feta and stir to thoroughly combine. Remove the filo pastry from the packaging and lay onto a chopping board or clean worksurface. Cover with a damp towel so that it doesn't dry out too much.

Whisk the remaining 2 eggs with the remaining oil and season with a little salt. Oil the base and sides of a 25cm (10in) round cake tin and lay a sheet of filo on the bottom, bunching it up the sides of the tin. Brush the pastry with the egg and oil mixture and repeat with 3 more pastry sheets.

Carefully scrunch up 3 sheets of pastry to create layers and arrange in the tin. Sprinkle with a little sparkling water and cover with some of the egg and cheese mixture. Repeat until you have 3 sheets of pastry left. Layer the final 3 sheets of pasty into the tin, brushing each with the egg and oil mixture, to create a crust. Bake in the oven for 45 minutes.

Allow to cool for 5 minutes before carefully removing the pie and placing it on 4–5 upturned glasses to allow the steam to release and to ensure the bottom is crisp. Allow to cool for 15 minutes before slicing.

Gibanica Breakfast Plate

This is a great way to use up Gibanica (opposite). It's a match made in Balkan heaven of jammy egg yolks, creamy cheese, salty sausages, and your favourite hot sauce. Go all out and own this power breakfast platter; replace the meat with vegetarian sausages if you like, add a couple of hash browns if you're hungover; you could poach your eggs instead, you could add bacon... Most importantly, find pleasure in sharing the beginning of a new day with friends or family, whenever you can.

SERVES 4

4 sausages

¼ quantity Gibanica (see opposite)
    cut into 5cm (2in) chunks

Vegetable or sunflower oil, for frying

4 eggs

150g (5½oz) ricotta

Salt

To serve

1 quantity marinated red peppers
    (follow the recipe for Mum's
    Courgette's on page 116, using red
    peppers in place of the courgettes/
    zucchini)

Pomegranate Hot Sauce (see page
    29) or store-bought hot sauce
    (optional)

Preheat the grill (broiler) and cook the sausages according to the instructions on the packet. Five minutes before the end of the cooking time, add the Gibanica pie chunks to the tray with the sausages to warm through and toast slightly.

Heat a little oil in a frying pan over a medium heat and fry the eggs. Eggs are a personal matter, but I fry mine for about 3 minutes and then remove the pan from the heat, allowing the whites to cook slowly but completely and leaving the egg yolk soft and jammy.

Using the photograph overleaf as a guide, assemble the ingredients on a serving platter. Top with the ricotta so that it melts a little and add a sprinkling of salt.

Photographed on pages 96–97.

Meze
and Salata

Welcome to the Kafana

Kafana, our version of bistros or tavernas, are a Balkan institution with a culture of their own. They are the pillars of each community they reside in. In North Macedonia there are over five thousand of them and in a country of just over one million, this should give you a sense of how integral they are to our way of life. The pricing is accessible, the décor is down to earth, and you can really let loose in these spaces with no judgement passed by their owners as long as you can hold yourself together enough to sit up-right in your chair. Inevitably, this gave them a bad reputation, as alluded to in the popular music of Yugoslavia from the 70's and 80's. Branded as dive bars for drunks, gamblers, and shady businessmen, songs about people getting so inebriated they'd smash the glasses all around them emerged and with it came the stigma. But they've never stopped serving and welcome every kind of person.

In seeking out the most traditional kind of kafana to immerse myself in while trying to define what it is that makes them so special, I found Toni. Toni owns Frosina just outside Skopje city centre, named after his wife, the head chef. An intimate place, it has the feel of someone's dining room; little wooden tables

pushed together, red checked tablecloths, the old boys outside with their ashtrays and small jugs of Mastika (an aniseed based liquor) at 2pm. It's the kind of place where you feel rude not greeting everyone as you walk in and I'm ushered to a table of family and friends, one arm already around my shoulders. Toni is a professional at a warm welcome, his popularity obvious as passers-by shout his name through the open windows.

There are already plates of half-eaten meze at the table; this is normal as whoever arrives first will start ordering, then you sit down and do the same and so on, with each person taking their time but always eating something, the most honest reason being so that they can carry on drinking. First salty meze and fresh salads followed by breads and meats, relishes and pickles. Nothing feels quite like a starter or main and definitely not a small plate – just a natural, ebb and flow of food and no rush to turn the tables.

Some places have live music at the weekends, normally someone on a keyboard with a microphone which is rendered useless as you can only hear the chorus of guests and their favourite folk songs. There's no music at Toni's; the focus is on the food, and they make as much of it as they can on the premises.

Seasonality and the quality of each ingredient is of utmost importance, and in a country where it's cheaper to buy directly from small artisan producers, they're unable to get more than a couple of jars of the only honey they'll use at a time. Then there's Frosina's family breeding the pigs that will end up in so many delicious dishes (my favourite being baked in a clay pot with a mountain of leeks). They even take pre-orders for entertaining at home, packaged-up and ready to go, for those that don't have the time to cook, unlike the women who created these ancient recipes and would have spent so much of their time in their own kitchens. They also make big batches of mekici to be collected by young families who don't want to deal with the dough, and they are open seven days a week, 9–1am, although I'm not so sure this closing time is always adhered to. Corba (soup), most commonly made from tripe, is served with bread to cure heavy heads in the morning; I notice a table of sunglasses nearby at a questionable 3pm, doing just that.

Toni and I bond over our hustle and our thirst to keep going through the hardest of times, neither of us particularly seeking fame or fortune but just a happy life, bursting at the seams with people enjoying our hospitality and our commitment to good food. There is, however, a darker tone to our conversation. If the younger generation aren't interested in coming to these places anymore – if they're looking to leave, to find greener grass, slowly disconnecting from the importance of continuing tradition – who will take these places over when the elders, who for the most part keep them going, are gone? It hits me hard as I've never thought of it that way before – will they simply not exist in a couple of decades' time?

The answer is that they must be preserved at all costs. Like a good British cafe or an independent, traditional pub, they offer something honest and are open to all. As we slip down into the abyss of every food establishment looking the same, everything feeling like an ad, or the success of food depending on it being Instagrammable, the very heart of society and culture is on its knees. It's so easy to take something that feels so every day for granted, but it might not be there anymore unless it's supported; a concept that makes me miss places like kafanas before they are even gone.

Shopska Salata

As much as we adore salads, this tomato, cucumber, onion, and cheese salad (sometimes with the addition of raw peppers) must be the most ordered, most eaten, and most spotted on restaurant tables. An expression of gorgeous simplicity.

This isn't the first time or the last that I'll push the idea of sticking to seasonality, truly there is no point in making this at any other time than summer, unless you can get your hands on some mighty fine winter tomatoes.

Simply find the best tomatoes you can, combine with cucumber and chopped raw white onion, olive oil, and salt, then finish with a mountain of brined white cheese. Divine.

SERVES 4

3 large, ripe tomatoes

½ large cucumber

½ white onion

150g (5½oz) feta or other white brined cheese, well-chilled

Olive oil and salt, to taste

Slice the tomatoes into 5cm (2in) chunks and place into a serving bowl.

Peel the cucumber, slice into 5cm (2in) chunks, and add to the serving bowl.

Finely dice the onion, add to the serving bowl, and dress generously with olive oil and salt to taste.

Grate the well-chilled cheese (keeping the cheese in the fridge until the very last minute will ensure it grates easily) and pile on top of the tomato, cucumber, and onion. Serve and enjoy!

Zelena Salata

I so appreciate this green salad (pronounced "zelehna"). I particularly love it with lasagne and chips, lamb chops and butter sauce, or on the side of a huge leek-heavy straight-off-the-grill Macedonian sausage. If it's on the menu and it looks like the restaurant might give it the attention it deserves, I'm ordering it. So much more than just lettuce, a good, green salad can be served throughout the year, confidently holding its own against any meal, not just lasagne and sausage.

SERVES 6

2 heads of soft butterhead lettuce
1 shallot, finely diced
1 stick of celery, peeled into ribbons
1 long green pepper
1 tbsp full-fat yogurt
1 tsp sesame oil
Zest and juice of 1 lemon
1 tbsp runny honey
Salt and freshly ground black pepper

To serve
Oil from on top of the Tomato Jam
   on page 33, or olive oil
1 tbsp store-bought crunchy fried
   onions

Arrange the lettuce leaves in a serving bowl. Combine the remaining ingredients in a jug (measuring cup) and whisk well. Pour the dressing over the lettuce leaves and toss lightly.

Drizzle with the tomato or olive oil, sprinkle over the crunchy onions and serve with Ultimate Musaka (see page 192).

Cucumber, Pickled Wild Garlic Oil, Thick Yogurt, Walnuts, and Honey

Go wild garlic picking! Found in shady woods and by marshes, you'll discover these sweet leaves in glorious abundance between the end of winter and the beginning of summer, so make your oil when you can. Sweeter than regular garlic, wild garlic carries notes of dewy spring fields, forests, and marshes. Although it's the buds that are usually pickled, this recipe is totally unique and tried, tested, and enjoyed by many of my customers. It's punchy and a little goes a long way.

Pickling the leaves takes three days and the yogurt takes 24 hours to strain, so this is one to prep in advance.

ABOUT 500ML (16FL OZ) OIL, SALAD SERVES 4

For the pickled wild garlic oil

120g (4¼oz) wild garlic leaves, roughly chopped

150g (5½oz) caster (superfine) sugar

1 tbsp salt

250ml (9fl oz) white wine vinegar

150ml (5fl oz) olive oil, plus extra for drizzling

For the salad

300g (10oz) full-fat yogurt

1 cucumber, sliced into ribbons

200g (7oz) ground walnuts

50ml (1¾fl oz) runny honey

Salt and freshly ground black pepper

To make the wild garlic oil, first pickle the leaves. Combine the leaves, sugar, salt, and vinegar in a small saucepan over a medium heat. Bring to the boil and cook for 5 minutes or until fully incorporated. Set aside to cool completely.

Transfer the garlic mixture to a blender or food processor and blend until smooth. Transfer to an airtight container and place in the fridge for 3 days.

Drain the garlic mixture through a fine sieve, discarding the liquid. Transfer to a blender or food processor, add the olive oil and blend to combine. The oil can be stored in the fridge for up to 2 weeks in an airtight container or 6 months in a sterilized jar (see page 21).

To make the salad, first strain the yogurt. Line a fine mesh sieve with muslin (cheesecloth) and place over a bowl. Place the yogurt into the sieve and refrigerate for 24 hours.

Transfer the yogurt to a bowl, season well, and drizzle with olive oil.

To serve, cover the bottom of a serving dish with the yogurt. Arrange the cucumber on the dish and season lightly with salt. Drizzle with the wild garlic oil, sprinkle over the walnuts and finish with the honey.

Snow White Salad with Green Olive and Anchovy Panzanella

Snow White Salad, or snezhanka salata, is most commonly served in Bulgaria; I'm guessing it takes its name from the purity of the yogurt used. Ideal for bites in between that first shot of something strong, singing notes of summer when paired with a well-soaked panzanella, or in winter, swapping out the fresh cucumber for crunchy pickles and serving it just as it is. I just love that we call so many creamy, opulent combinations "salata"; what a wonderful way to be.

SERVES 4–6

For the panzanella

200g (7oz) day-old sourdough, white tin loaf or focaccia

Olive oil, for drizzling

3 medium, ripe tomatoes

2 large garlic cloves, finely chopped

For the snow white salad

400g (14oz) labneh or thick Greek-style yogurt (the thicker the better)

100g (3½oz) feta or goat's cheese, crumbled

½ cucumber, finely diced

100g (3½oz) walnuts, finely chopped

1 bunch of dill, finely chopped

To assemble

1 soft butterhead lettuce or similar

Juice of ½ a lemon

50g (1¾oz) tinned anchovies

200g (7oz) pitted green olives (I use the anchovy- or garlic-stuffed ones)

Salt and freshly ground black pepper

At least 1 hour before serving, preheat the grill (broiler) to high and cut or tear the bread into chunks. Lay the bread onto a baking sheet, drizzle with olive oil and toast, turning once, until slightly charred and crispy all over. Transfer to a bowl.

If you're making this in the peak of summer, crush the tomatoes in your hands and coat the warm bread chunks with the tomato juice. If not, you may need to slice the tomatoes into chunks.

Add half of the garlic and a good drizzle of olive oil, and season to taste. Set aside for at least an hour to allow the bread to soak up the juices.

To make the snow white salad, add the yogurt, cheese, cucumber, walnuts, remaining garlic, and the dill to a bowl and mix well to combine. Drizzle with olive oil and season to taste – go easy on the salt as the cheese will be quite salty. Set aside, ideally for no longer than an hour (any longer is fine but you may need to spoon off any liquid that rises to the surface).

To assemble, arrange the torn lettuce on a serving plate and dress lightly with a drizzle of olive oil, the lemon juice, and a little more salt if needed. Layer the soaked bread, anchovies, and olives (I slice half of the olives and anchovies and leave the rest whole, but it's up to you how you present it) onto the lettuce leaves and top with the snow white salad. Finish with a final drizzle of olive oil.

Photographed on page 114.

Mum's Courgettes with Courgette Tartar

Many people from many different cultures instantly fill up with warmth at the thought of a matriarch or elder carefully removing food from sizzling oil and laying it out on kitchen paper, usually on a cramped kitchen surface, with a hand slapping away anyone who tries to take a bite before it's ready.

For me, this vision is summers in Skopje. Someone would ask "what are we having for dinner today?" and we would all agree "let's just have courgettes". JUST courgette, as if going to the outside oven and standing over a pool of hot oil, surrounded by scorched air, sweating, carefully inspecting with an equally hot fork, turning, lifting, dropping, sometimes blistering, was no labour of love or a massive effort.

With vinegar, garlic, parsley, and salt, this classic technique is a champion side dish and used for lots of different vegetables, including aubergine (eggplant) and (bell) peppers. We would eat it as a family with white cheese, bread to mop up the juices, and maybe some cold ajvar, too. My mum makes this dish the best and, although it is a common celebration of summer, I've always thought of it as hers, served here with my courgette tartar.

The courgette tartar is best prepared a few hours before serving. Do bear in mind that the longer it keeps, the more juices will be released and the thinner the dip will be – it's definitely best eaten within two days.

SERVES 4

For the tartar
1 small courgette (zucchini), very finely diced

1 small red onion, finely diced

Handful of parsley, finely chopped

Handful of dill, finely chopped

4 gherkins (small pickles), finely chopped

50g (1¾oz) capers, roughly chopped

Zest and juice of 1 lemon

130g (4¾oz) soured cream

100g (3½oz) full-fat mayonnaise

Drizzle of olive oil

Salt and freshly ground black pepper

For the courgettes
2 large courgettes (zucchini; the bigger the better)

About 3 tbsp vegetable or sunflower oil, for frying

1 large garlic clove, finely chopped

Handful of parsley, finely chopped

2 tbsp white wine, apple cider or balsamic vinegar

Photographed on page 115.

To make the courgette tartar, combine all the ingredients together in a bowl and set aside.

To make the courgettes, slice the courgettes into 1.5cm (½in) discs.

Heat 1.5 tbsp of the oil in a wide frying pan over a medium heat. Fry the courgettes until golden brown on both sides and place on a clean tea towel or kitchen paper (paper towel) to drain. Work in batches, adding more oil as needed (ensure the oil is hot before adding the courgettes).

Return the courgettes to the pan, add the remaining ingredients with a pinch of salt and mix well.

Serve the courgettes with the tartar on the side. The tartar is also delicious with a big bowl of crisps for dipping or as a summer side dish.

Malidzano and Candied Jalapeños

Derived from the Italian word melanzane, this Macedonian take on an aubergine dip is unique in that it uses mustard – not a common combination. It's sometimes referred to as "green ajvar".

You can use green or red peppers, depending on the colour you want to achieve, and if you can't handle the heat, just omit the jalapeños. This is great served with chips (see page 154) or really good crisps.

SERVES 4

For the candied jalapeños
50ml (1¾fl oz) white wine vinegar
20g (¾oz) caster (superfine) sugar
3 jalapeños, thinly sliced

For the malidzano
1 large aubergine (eggplant)
6 long green peppers
1 large garlic clove
1 tbsp Dijon mustard
1¼ tbsp vegetable oil
½ bunch of parsley
50g (1¾oz) ground walnuts

To make the candied jalapeños, add the vinegar and sugar to a small non-stick saucepan over a medium heat and cook, stirring, until completely combined.

Add the jalapeños and cook, stirring occasionally, for about 5 minutes or until the jalapeños appear shiny and most of the liquid has evaporated. Set aside to cool.

To make the malidzano, char the aubergine by carefully holding it over the flames of your gas hob, or place under a grill (broiler) heated to the highest setting, turning often, until it is almost entirely blackened and softened. Immediately transfer to a plastic bag or large plastic container with a lid, sealing the bag or closing the lid – this will make the peeling process easier. Leave the aubergine in the sealed bag or covered container for about an hour or set aside until the following day.

Half fill a large bowl with water. Remove the aubergine from the bag or container and carefully remove the charred skin, discarding the skin and dipping your hands in the water as you go to clean them. Roughly chop the aubergine. A little juice will be left in the bag or container – I like to add this to the pan with the jalapeños for flavour but you can discard it if you prefer.

Transfer the aubergine to a blender or food processor and add the remaining ingredients (the long green peppers can go in whole). Blend until smooth.

Place the malidzano into a bowl and pile the candied jalapeños on top. Serve with pide, pitta bread, or crisps for dipping.

Breaded Olives and Battered Aubergine

This is a classic kafana staple, hot crunchy nibbles dotted around any respectable daska (mezze board) and used on page 143. Don't scrimp on the olives, find the juiciest you can. Immediately close this book if you even considered using the those little, pitted, rubbery ones, you know the ones you get on cheap pizza – those are practically non-olives to me. Although we don't have the same climate to grow the magnificent olives of North Macedonia, a good olive is not hard to find, so look for something big and juicy – black or green will do.

SERVES 4

1 aubergine (eggplant), thinly sliced

2 tbsp salt

350g (12oz) best-quality olives, pitted

120g (4¼oz) gram flour (Besan; chickpea flour)

300ml (10fl oz) vegetable oil, for frying

50g (1¾oz) plain (all-purpose) flour

50g (1¾oz) fine breadcrumbs

1 egg, whisked

Salt and freshly ground black pepper

To serve

Courgette Tartar (see page 116)

Lemon wedges

Place the aubergine slices into a colander set over a bowl. Cover with the 2 tbsp salt and set aside for 1 hour to allow any excess liquid to drain.

Meanwhile, drain the olives and pat them dry using kitchen paper (paper towel).

Whisk the gram flour and about 50ml (1¾fl oz) cold water together to form a batter. You may need slightly more or less water to achieve a smooth consistency. Season.

Heat the oil in a large saucepan over a medium heat for 8 minutes. Meanwhile place the plain flour, breadcrumbs, egg, and batter into separate bowls, seasoning as you go.

Dip the olives into the flour, followed by the egg and finally the breadcrumbs. Carefully lower the olives into the oil and cook for about 3 minutes or until golden brown. Move them around so they cook evenly and don't overcrowd the pan. Drain the olives on kitchen paper (paper towel).

Coat the aubergine slices in the flour and then dip into the batter, shaking gently to remove any excess. Carefully lower into the oil and fry for about 4 minutes or until golden brown, flipping them over once or twice as they cook. Drain on kitchen paper and season.

Serve with the Courgette Tartar and a squeeze of lemon.

Cheese Piroshki

A familiar recipe to many countries, this stuffed and fried potato dough has a tonne of variations in North Macedonia alone. Some make it with minced meat or ham and cheese, some without potato, and some leave it plain for crucial plate mopping or for soaking up too many drinks. Piroshkis remind me of being dragged to loud parties as a kid, piles of them on silver platters, squeezing as many as I could into my little belly while the tables wobbled with the rhythm of clapping and dancing around me, the cutlery playing its own beat.

This recipe comes from Prilep, a town in the southwest of the country. I use traditional kashkaval cheese, which you can find in the Polish section of most large supermarkets, or you can use any melty cheese you fancy, such as Gouda or mild Cheddar. Serve in any situation that deserves good snacking.

MAKES 12

100ml (3½fl oz) milk

7g (¼oz) packet fast action yeast

Pinch of sugar

500g (1lb 2oz) potatoes, peeled and cubed

3 eggs, whisked, plus 2 yolks

2 tbsp salt, plus extra for seasoning

Freshly ground black pepper

About 300g (10oz) plain (all-purpose) flour

400g (14oz) fine breadcrumbs

400ml (14fl oz) vegetable or sunflower oil

200g (7oz) kashkaval, Gouda, or mild Cheddar, grated

To serve

Lemon wedges

Courgette Tartar (see page 116) or mayonnaise

Photographed on page 122.

Gently heat the milk until it's lukewarm to touch – be careful to not overheat it or it will kill the yeast. Combine the yeast, pinch of sugar, and the warm milk in a jug. Cover with a tea towel and set aside in a warm place for 10–15 minutes or until frothy.

Meanwhile, boil the potatoes until soft – don't overcook them as they may end up too watery for the dough. Drain the potatoes and mash them until they're completely smooth. Set aside to cool.

Pour the yeast mixture into the cooled potatoes and stir to combine with a spatula or wooden spoon. Add the egg yolks, 1¼ tbsp lukewarm water, the salt, and plenty of black pepper. Stir to combine then gradually add the flour, stirring to combine after each addition. Use your hands to bring the mixture together to form a sticky dough that comes away from the bowl when you pull at it. If not, add a little more flour. Transfer the dough to a well-oiled bowl, cover with a tea towel and leave in a warm place for about 1 hour.

Meanwhile put the breadcrumbs onto a large plate. Pour the whisked eggs onto a separate plate and season both.

Turn the dough out onto a well-floured surface – the dough will be sticky so also flour your hands and rolling pin. Divide the dough in 2 and roll each half into a long sausage shape, about 5cm (2in) thick. Divide each sausage shape into 6 and roll each piece into a ball. Transfer to a well-oiled baking sheet, cover with a tea towel and set aside for 10 minutes.

Add the oil to a wide saucepan large enough to submerge half of the piroshki and place over a low-medium heat (you may need to tweak the temperature as you go to ensure the piroshki aren't browning too quickly).

Meanwhile, roll out each dough ball to the thickness of fresh pasta. Spoon about 15g (½oz) of the cheese onto the centre of the dough, leaving a little room around the edges, then fold over the bottom of the dough, covering the cheese completely, and gently pinch in to close. Do the same for the sides: fold in and pinch down to close. Finally, roll the dough over – much like a burrito – and roll up, pinching again to close. You can gently re-mould if needed to get an even, fat cigar shape, just be careful to not break the dough. Repeat for each of the rolled-out dough balls.

To check if the oil is ready, take a pinch of dough and drop it into the oil. If the oil is hot enough the dough should immediately start bubbling and rise to the surface. If not, heat the oil for a little longer and repeat the test.

Carefully dip each piroshki into the whisked egg, allowing any excess to drip off, then gently roll each one in the breadcrumbs. You can either breadcrumb all the piroshki now or fry the first one and breadcrumb each one as you go – whatever you feel comfortable with.

Gently drop the piroshki into the oil and fry for 3–4 minutes, turning a couple of times to ensure they are evenly golden brown. Remove from the pan and drain on kitchen paper (paper towel).

Serve with lemon wedges, Courgette Tartar or a dollop of good mayonnaise.

Mortadela Piroshki with Feta Sauce

Drop an 'L' from the Italian mortadella and you've got the Balkan name for the fatty ham that is produced across the whole region: mortadela. Although its origins lie in Bologna, it's popular throughout the Balkans. It's salty and coats your mouth in fat that melts like butter. This means it's great for meze, served on a board with cheeses and pickles, or, for me, eaten at the kitchen counter, folded into parcels of sweet bliss. Stuffing it into deep-fried Piroshki warms it through, releasing the rich, meaty flavour into the pastry.

MAKES 12

For the piroshki
400g (14oz) mortadella, very finely sliced into 12 slices
1 quantity Cheese Piroshki dough (see page 120 – omit the cheese)

For the feta sauce
150g (5½oz) feta
200ml (7fl oz) full-fat crème fraîche
Handful of parsley
Handful of tarragon
2 garlic cloves

Follow the recipe for Cheese Piroshki on page 120 to the point where the dough is rolled at the beginning of step 7. Slice the mortadella into 12 slices and use each slice to stuff each of the piroshkis in place of the Gouda or Cheddar, bunching the mortadella as you go to create layers. Continue with the recipe on page 120 to finish the piroshki.

To make the feta sauce, simply blend all of the ingredients together in a blender or food processor.

To serve, drizzle the sauce over the piroshki or serve on the side for dipping.

Photographed on page 123.

Balkan Potato Party

You'd be hard pushed to find a Balkan bash without a vat of Ruska salata (Russian salad) on the table. Hours are invested in dicing each ingredient as small as possible, and it's made with smoked ham for Christmas – a dish that most will say they're ready to see the back of once the new year and all the parties have finally passed. There are enough recipes for that on the internet, so this is a variation that still honours the beauty found in heavy helpings of mayonnaise and boiled potatoes. It's best made the day before serving.

SERVES 6

For the dressing

200g (7oz) brined white cheese or feta, crumbled

100g (3½oz) soured cream

1 tbsp wholegrain mustard

100g (3½oz) mayonnaise

Zest and juice of 1 lemon

2 tbsp white wine vinegar

3 tbsp olive oil

For the salad

700g (1½lb) potatoes, cubed, boiled and cooled

4 hardboiled eggs, cooled and chopped

3 red or green peppers, thinly sliced

2 spring onions (scallions), thinly sliced, plus extra to serve

4 pickled gherkins (small pickles), finely chopped

3 tbsp chopped walnuts

Salt and freshly ground black pepper

1 bunch of parsley, roughly chopped, to serve

Combine all the dressing ingredients in a bowl or jug (measuring cup). Season to taste and set aside.

Arrange the potatoes, eggs, peppers, spring onions, pickles, and walnuts in a serving bowl. Spoon the dressing over and stir gently until well combined. Cover with cling film (plastic wrap) and refrigerate until ready to serve.

Stir in the parsley, sprinkle over the extra spring onion, check the seasoning, and serve.

Crispy White Fish with Basil Mayo and Slatko – Kora od Lubenica

I've eaten plenty of fried fish in North Macedonia, usually out of paper and brought home by someone who picked it out for the fishmonger to fry. Most notable is whole European hake or trout lightly fried in plenty of salt and a little flour. Being a landlocked country with the gorgeous Lake Ohrid that borders Albania, lake fish reign supreme.

However, it's the UK that has my heart when it comes to sitting in fish and chip shops – watching the pounding rain hit the window, basking in the steam that hits my frozen face while adding lashings of vinegar to battered cod and chunky chips.

This dish is great on its own as a starter or snack, but you can make it a main serving with Crunchy Potatoes (see page 132). I like to use Thomy or any Polish mayo you can find in most big supermarkets, but if you like you can swap out the basil mayo for my Courgette Tartar (see page 116), adding a splash of vinegar at the end for a more authentic chip-shop taste.

SERVES 4

For the mayo
1 bunch of basil
1 garlic clove
100g (3½oz) full-fat mayonnaise
Juice of 1 lemon

For the fish
80g (2¾oz) plain (all purpose) flour
1 tsp baking powder
200g (7oz) firm white fish fillet, such as cod or hake, sliced into 5cm (2in) chunks
200ml (7fl oz) vegetable or sunflower oil, for frying
Salt and freshly ground black pepper

To serve
Handful of dill, chopped
5 pieces of Slatko – Kora od Lubenica (see page 24), quartered
Lemon juice or vinegar (optional)

To make the mayo, simply add all the ingredients to a blender or food processor and blend to combine. Set aside to allow the flavours to develop.

To make the batter, sift the flour and baking powder together and transfer to a large bowl. Gradually pour in 100ml (3½fl oz) cold water, a little at a time, whisking constantly to form a smooth batter. Season and set aside.

Carefully pat the fish with kitchen paper (paper towel) to remove any excess liquid, taking care not to break up the fish.

Heat the oil in a large wide saucepan over a medium heat for 8 minutes. The oil should fill to a depth of about 1cm (½in) so you may need to add a little more depending on the size of your pan. Test to see if the oil is hot enough by dropping a little batter into the oil – if it floats and becomes crispy, it's ready. If not, heat for a little longer and repeat the test.

Gently dip the fish into the batter, making sure it's completely covered. Shake gently to remove any excess (although I like to leave a little extra so that it becomes super crunchy when frying).

Fry the fish for about 3 minutes or until golden brown, turning regularly. Drain on kitchen paper.

Smother a serving plate with the mayo and place the fried fish on top. Garnish with dill and the watermelon rind, and drizzle with lemon or vinegar to finish (if using).

Photographed on pages 128–129.

Vegeta Chicken Wings

It's hard to put into words how crucial the seasoning Vegeta is in our cuisine. It sits at the backbone of most recipes, enhancing flavour since 1959 when it was created by a Bosnian Croat Scientist called Zlata Bartl, a hero of his time. You can find it in most supermarkets, and it's sold all over the world. I can't imagine my mum's kitchen without a jar of Vegeta above the cooker, and you can use it, even if it's not called for, as seasoning for pretty much any savoury recipe in this book. Some cooks may be a little snobby about it but there's no denying its long-lasting popularity; it's best to just give in to the power of Vegeta.

I was once served some fried chicken wings with nothing but a dusting of the magic seasoning on top in a traditional Macedonian restaurant; I haven't stopped thinking about them since, so here's my take on that dish. We salute you, Zlata.

SERVES 6

1kg (2¼lb) chicken wings, separated into drums and flats (drumettes and wingettes)

2 tbsp Vegeta seasoning, plus extra to serve

2 tbsp ground turmeric

Vegetable or sunflower oil, for frying

2 medium onions, finely chopped

About 300ml (10fl oz) white wine vinegar

1 bunch of parsley, finely chopped

Handful of store-bought fried, dried onion

Juice of 1 lemon

Place the chicken into a bowl and sprinkle over the Vegeta and turmeric. Toss to coat, cover, and refrigerate for around 3 hours, removing from the fridge 30 minutes before cooking.

Heat a little oil in a frying pan over a low heat. Add the onions and a splash of the vinegar. Stir until the vinegar has reduced and continue adding the vinegar and stirring until all the vinegar has been used and the onions are soft and translucent, about 10–15 minutes. Set aside in a large bowl.

Preheat the oven to 200°C (180°C fan/400°F/Gas 6). Line a baking tray with baking paper, toss the wings in a little oil and bake for around 40 minutes or until cooked through and the skin is super crispy.

Transfer the wings to the bowl with the softened onions and add the parsley, dried onion, lemon juice, and a generous sprinkle of Vegeta, and toss to combine thoroughly.

Crunchy Potatoes
with Fried Pepper Cream

This dish is perfect for a low-key TV dinner or a more crowded table kind of affair. The peppers will spit as they cook so treat yourself to a mesh cover for your frying pan; such a staple in most immigrant homes.

SERVES 4

Vegetable or sunflower oil, for frying

4 sweet, red pointed peppers (such as Romano)

4 long green peppers

For the pepper cream

2 red (bell) peppers, roughly chopped

1 green (bell) pepper, roughly chopped

4 pickled onions

200ml (7fl oz) crème fraîche

Salt and freshly ground black pepper

For the onion dressing

1 bunch of spring onions (scallions), finely sliced

12 pickled onions, finely sliced

1 bunch of parsley, finely chopped

2 tsp olive oil

Salt, to taste

For the crunchy potatoes

500g (1lb 2oz) new potatoes

300ml (10fl oz) vegetable oil

Heat a little oil in a large frying pan over a medium heat. Add the 4 long green peppers and 4 red pointed peppers and fry until starting to soften, about 5–8 minutes. Transfer the peppers to an airtight container or cover them in cling film (plastic wrap) and set aside for 20 minutes to soften.

To make the pepper cream, place all the ingredients into a food processor or blender and blend until smooth. Season with salt and pepper and set aside in the fridge to set (this can be done up to a day in advance).

Transfer the whole peppers to a bowl and add the onion dressing ingredients. Toss gently to combine and set aside.

To make the crunchy potatoes, boil the potatoes in a large saucepan for 10–15 minutes or until tender but not falling apart. Drain and set aside to cool completely.

Heat the measured oil in a large saucepan over a medium-high heat for 8 minutes.

Gently press down on each potato with your hands so that they flatten but don't fall apart. Carefully drop the potatoes into the oil and fry for 5 minutes or until super crispy, turning halfway and working in batches as needed and avoiding overcrowding the pan. Drain the potatoes on kitchen paper (paper towel).

Remove the cream from the fridge and top with the dressed peppers. Serve with the crunchy potatoes.

Fried Green Tomatoes, Fudgy Eggs, Tomato Jam, and Chervil Mayo

I became obsessed with the notion of frying green tomatoes after watching the 1991 film with the same title, starring Kathy Bates. As a child I was taken with the notion of these two best friends running a café together, blocking out the darker themes in the story. So here I'm using green tomatoes to celebrate the friendships I have made while running my own business, and eggs because no meze platter is complete without them.

SERVES 4

1 bunch of chervil

100g (3½oz) mayonnaise

Juice of ½ lime

200ml (7fl oz) vegetable oil, for frying

100g (3½oz) plain (all-purpose) flour

2 eggs, whisked

100g (3½oz) fine breadcrumbs

4 medium green tomatoes, cut into 1cm (½in) slices

3 hardboiled eggs

Salt and freshly ground black pepper

To serve

Tomato Jam (see page 33)

Olive oil, for drizzling

Add half of the chervil to a food processor or blender with the mayonnaise and lime juice. Season with salt and pepper and blend until combined. Cover and set aside.

Heat the oil in a large saucepan over a medium heat for 8 minutes. Meanwhile, place the flour, whisked egg, and breadcrumbs in separate bowls and season well. First dunk the tomato slices in the flour, then egg, then finally the breadcrumbs.

Carefully drop the coated tomato slices into the oil and fry for 3–4 minutes or until golden brown, turning halfway. Work in batches as needed and don't overcrowd the pan. Drain on a tea towel or kitchen paper (paper towel).

Meanwhile, peel the hardboiled eggs and slice each in half. Arrange the mayo, eggs, and dollops of Tomato Jam on a serving plate. Season the eggs and top with the hot tomato slices, sprigs of the remaining chervil and a drizzle of olive oil.

Cauliflower Turšija Fritters

with Soured Cream and 'Nduja Dip

This recipe takes the Turšija on page 36 and elevates it to new heights with a spicy 'nduja dip. 'Nduja is a sweet and spicy cured Italian sausage sold in many supermarkets and Italian delis. If you are struggling to find it then chorizo is a good substitute. The soured cream perfectly cools off the tangy heat from the sausage and the tartness from the pickles. Cauliflower is a stellar choice for this; there's something about the texture as you bite through and the level of coverage you get with the dip. For a vegetarian version, just swap out the 'nduja for the same quantity of Tomato Jam (see page 33) and add a pinch of dried chilli.

SERVES 4

For the dip

Vegetable or sunflower oil, for frying

1 small red onion, roughly chopped

2 garlic cloves, roughly chopped

300g (10oz) 'nduja, skin removed if necessary

Zest and juice of 1 lemon

2½ tbsp honey

200ml (7fl oz) soured cream

For the fritters

500g (1lb 2oz) cauliflower Turšija (see page 36), drained

400ml (14fl oz) vegetable or sunflower oil

3 eggs

140g (5oz) cornflour (cornstarch), sifted

2 tsp baking powder

1 tbsp dried dill

Salt and freshly ground black pepper

To make the dip, heat a little oil in a frying pan over a medium heat. Add the onion and fry, stirring occasionally, until golden brown and softened. Add the garlic, stir to combine and cook for 30 seconds. Remove the pan from the heat and allow the onion and garlic to cool.

Add the cooled onion and garlic to a blender or food processor along with the remaining ingredients and blitz until smooth. Set the dip aside until ready to serve. If you're making the dip ahead of time, set aside in the fridge and bring to room temperature to serve so it's extra dippable.

To make the fritters, pat the cauliflower turšija dry using kitchen paper (paper towel). Heat the oil in a deep, wide saucepan over a medium heat for 8 minutes.

Break the eggs into a bowl. Blend 100g (3½oz) of the cornflour with a little water to form a paste, then gradually whisk into the eggs along with the baking powder, dill, and seasoning. Set aside.

Toss the cauliflower in the remaining 40g (1½oz) of cornflour for about 30 seconds, then immerse in the egg mixture.

To test if the oil is hot enough, drop in a little of the egg mixture – if it floats and crisps-up, it's ready.

Remove the cauliflower from the egg mixture, draining any excess batter, and carefully place the florets into the hot oil using a slotted spoon or tongs. Work in batches as needed and don't overcrowd the saucepan or the fritters will lose their crunch.

Fry the cauliflower for around 4 minutes, turning occasionally, until light golden brown. Carefully remove using a slotted spoon or tongs and drain on kitchen paper.

Serve the cauliflower fritters with the 'nduja dip on the side, and let the dipping commence.

Sticky Onion Dolma

We tend to think of dolma as a dish of stuffed vine leaves, but the word actually refers to a whole family of stuffed vegetables, leaves, fruits, or offal, and is associated with anywhere that was once a part of the Ottoman Empire. As a region that celebrates the art of wine making, vine leaves are in abundance and recipe variations call for meat, eaten as a main, or a vegetarian version served at room temperature as meze (see photograph on pages 144–145). This vegan take on the classic is all about the onions; once you realize the difference it makes to cook them low and slow while stirring, showering them in the attention they deserve, you'll never look back.

Vine leaves in brine can be bought from most Mediterranean or Middle Eastern supermarkets or online. The weight I've given is approximate; I ended up with 27 leaves I could use for stuffing and the rest for lining the baking dish, but you may have a few more or less. This is a great dish to prepare in advance and also freezes really well.

MAKES ABOUT 27

350g (12oz) long-grain rice, well rinsed

Vegetable or sunflower oil, for frying

10 medium onions, thinly sliced or finely chopped in a food processor

3 lemons

5 garlic cloves, finely chopped

2 tsp caster (superfine) sugar or 4 tbsp honey

50ml (1¾fl oz) white wine vinegar or apple cider vinegar

2 tbsp pomegranate molasses

2 tbsp ground cumin

500g (1lb 2oz) vine leaves in brine

100g (3½oz) walnuts, finely chopped

Olive oil, for drizzling

2 tbsp Vegeta seasoning

Salt and freshly ground black pepper

Pour the rice into a medium saucepan and add twice the volume of water. Place the pan over a medium heat and bring to the boil. Stir once, reduce the heat to low, cover, and cook for about 10 minutes or according to the instructions on the packet. Separate the rice using a fork and set aside.

Heat a splash of oil in a large saucepan over a medium-low heat. Add the onions and cook, stirring continuously to prevent them from catching, until softened. Add a splash of water and the juice and zest of 2 of the lemons. Cook for about 10 minutes, stirring continuously.

Add 100ml (3½fl oz) water, 1 tbsp at a time, stirring after each addition until the onions have absorbed the water. Cook for a further 25 minutes, stirring continuously.

Add the garlic, honey, vinegar, pomegranate molasses, cumin, and a little salt and continue to cook for a further 20 minutes, or until the onions are glossy and slightly sticky, stirring continuously. Set aside.

To prepare the vine leaves, carefully remove them from the jar and place in a large saucepan. Cover with water, place the pan over a medium heat and bring to the boil. Cook for 10–12 minutes, then drain and set aside to cool.

Set aside the large, intact leaves that are suitable for stuffing – any smaller or broken leaves can be used to line the baking tray.

Tip the cooled onions and walnuts into the rice and season well.

Preheat the oven to 160°C (140°C fan/325°F/Gas 3). Line a 30cm (12in) baking tray with the smaller or broken vine leaves and drizzle with olive oil (if you're using a smaller, deeper dish you may need to layer the stuffed vine leaves on top of each other later).

Spoon 2 tbsp of the rice mixture into the bottom centre of each of the larger vine leaves and then fold in the sides. Roll the leaves up from the bottom and tuck in each end. You may need to adjust the amount of rice mixture depending on the size of the leaves – you want to be able to roll them up neatly but make sure they're not over-stuffed or they will burst. Arrange the stuffed vine leaves on the lined baking tray, packing them as tightly as you can.

Chop the remaining lemon into chunks and tuck in between the leaves. Mix the Vegeta with 250ml (9fl oz) water and pour over the vine leaves. Cover with foil and bake for an hour and a half, or until the water has evaporated.

Drizzle the dolma with olive oil as soon as it comes out of the oven and serve immediately, or cool and store in the fridge for up to 3 days.

Hibiscus Salmon, Pickle, and Whipped Cream Cheese Platter

Much like recipes for beetroot-cured salmon, hibiscus honours the fish with its dreamy pink hue. This is ideal for serving to guests as it is or stuffed into a dense bagel. The fish will be ready to eat in two days and should be eaten within five.

SERVES 4–6

2 tbsp salt

2 tbsp caster (superfine) sugar

2 handfuls of dried hibiscus

2 skinless salmon fillets

To serve

200g (7oz) full-fat cream cheese

Hibiscus Pickles with Pistachios (see page 38)

Handful of chopped pistachios

Olive oil, for drizzling

Add 300ml (10fl oz) water, the salt, sugar, and hibiscus to a saucepan over a medium heat. Stir and bring to the boil. Boil for 10 minutes, then set aside to cool completely.

Place the salmon into an airtight container, pour over the cooled liquid, cover, and refrigerate for 2 days.

When you are ready to serve, drain the salmon, slice very thinly, and whip the cream cheese until completely smooth.

Arrange the salmon slices on a serving platter. Either transfer the cream cheese to a piping bag and pipe it over the salmon, or just dollop it over. Scatter with the pickles and pistachios, and drizzle with olive oil.

Sesame Onion Rings

with Tarragon Honey Mustard

When visiting North Macedonia I'm inclined to grab a snack wherever I can, afraid to return to the UK with a sense of missing out on the snacks I didn't try. On a particularly hot day while researching this book, I stopped at a bar in the centre of Skopje, lured in by the free Wi-Fi but afraid of ultimately falling into a tourist trap. I was wrong about both; the Wi-Fi didn't work but the portions were huge (a Balkan standard) and, unable to check my emails, I fell into a big pile of onion rings, coated with crunchy sesame seeds and washed down with plenty of honey mustard and a cold larger. Genius.

SERVES 4

For the tarragon honey mustard

4 tbsp runny honey

2 tbsp Dijon mustard

½ bunch tarragon, leaves picked

For the sesame onion rings

1 large onion, thinly sliced into rings

2 tsp salt

300ml (10fl oz) vegetable oil

1 egg

1 tsp baking powder

100ml (3½fl oz) full-fat (whole) milk

6 tbsp plain (all-purpose) flour

4 tbsp toasted sesame seeds

To make the tarragon honey mustard, add the honey, mustard, and tarragon to a blender or food processor and blend to combine. Season with salt and set aside.

To make the onion rings, add the onion to a colander set over a bowl and cover with the salt. Set aside for 10 minutes.

Meanwhile heat the oil in a large wide saucepan over a medium heat for 8 minutes.

Whisk the egg, baking powder, milk, and flour together in a bowl with 3 tbsp of the sesame seeds to form a batter.

Once the oil is ready, shake any excess liquid from the onion slices and dip them in the batter, shaking off any excess. The sesame seeds tend to sink to the bottom of the batter, so stir it as you go.

Carefully drop the onion slices into the oil and fry for 2–3 minutes or until super crispy, working in batches as needed and taking care not to overcrowd the pan. Drain on kitchen paper (paper towel).

To serve, drizzle the onions with the tarragon honey mustard and sprinkle with the remaining sesame seeds.

Daska of Dreams

The best platters can be found at parties and this joyous way of eating spans cultures. The top tier plates feature mac and cheese, dumplings, and oxtail stew or dodo, suya, and chin chin. If you're smart, always bring a box to take extras home with you. Wow your guests with the same feeling I get when I see a daska (or meze board) so heavy, it takes a couple of waiting staff at the kafana to bring it over to the table.

This isn't a strict recipe but a guide – a daska suggestion of sorts. Use the photograph overleaf as inspiration and pick and choose from this chapter, adding whatever takes your fancy.

SERVES 2

Cheese Piroshki (see page 120)

Breaded Olives and Battered Aubergine (see page 119)

Sweet Tea Pickles (see page 25)

Courgette Tartar (see page 116)

Sticky Onion Dolma (see page 138)

Boiled eggs

Serrano ham

Manchego

Photographed on pages 144–145.

Глад.
јаде

Mains for Feasting

Tables Full of Love

The art of hosting Macedonian-style could be a book in its own right, a story of our generosity and thirst to please others through the offer of food and a well-laid table. Every person I've met while creating this book has left me with the feeling that we'd known each other our whole lives, a familiarity that is down to a shared passion to feed and be fed.

My memories from these encounters and beyond are centred around cluttered tables and mountains of food – a home-cooked meal waiting for me no matter the time I arrived from the airport – or being served slatko and a glass of water as soon as I sat down. It's a case of always putting the effort in, whether it be a special occasion or I only popped in for a coffee but that quickly turned into glasses of ouzo and a tornado of energy in the kitchen.

I've been entertained this way so many times, the result always being a respectable platter of meze or anything else from the kitchen; as a host you should be willing to share it all. Of course, the entertainment won't stop there; next is saying something ridiculous along the lines of "sorry it's not much," or "I should have brought more in" on repeat, not forgetting "yadi yadi!" which means "eat, eat!"

It's like these tables of food are etched into me; they've shaped me and made me who I am today. Of course, there's also my mum's spreads here in the UK. She always cooked enough to feed an army, and our fridge would be full of mysterious boxes of savoury and sweet leftovers for days afterwards.

It's dawned on me how central these meals are to our traditions, mostly tied to either the Orthodox Christian calendar or the Islamic calendar (the most prominent religions in North Macedonia). Those that have the willpower for lent and those who don't will put on a spread of vegetarian food on Badnik (Christmas Eve), dishes such as dolma, gravce tavce (a baked bean dish) and sometimes fish with ribnik. Not forgetting the essential loaf of soda bread with a coin baked into it, each person ripping away a chunk at the end of the night to find the money that will bring them luck for the next year. Christmas Day is heavy on meats, cheeses, pickles and beyond. For New Year's Eve no table is without a big bowl of Balkan potato party and most people go to the effort of making sarma.

At funerals, or 30 days after someone has passed (when it's believed the soul leaves our world for good) many people bring baked goods to the church ceremony, and the host's house will

be adorned with piles of pastries and the like. It's key that you serve something that the person who has passed loved to eat at these ceremonies. At weddings there's an opportunity to impress with giant platters of piroshki.

Then there's more low-key occasions, such as my 23rd birthday. This was a gathering of only my closest friends and family but was still an excuse for my Uncle Kole to wheel a whole spit-roasted suckling pig over to where I was sitting, beaming with pride. Whatever has brought you together, whether you're dancing on top of a table or sat down eating at it, you can guarantee that there will almost always be a big chunk of cheese, some good olives, and a bowl of ajvar.

It might sound corny to say that "I found myself through food" but it's true that I was lost for a very long time, and cooking for others, in a way that is inherently natural to me, has brought me a stronger sense of self. I feel it when I rush to find something to offer a guest when they arrive, or remembering to pick up something sweet for a loved one I'm visiting, or when I'm told, on repeat, how generous my portions are.

I show my love by chopping, kneading, slow cooking, and baking. There are also mystic moments while bathing in hospitality, sitting at someone else's table, hearing them make me a coffee or watching them look for something they really want me to try in the fridge. That's when it really sinks in and starts to make me feel whole; I guess I'm more Macedonian than I ever realized.

Kjufte with Hot Chips, Spicy Tomato Sos, and Cold Feta

For me, Balkan kjufte (a meat ball, pronounced "kyoofte") represent the comfort we find in togetherness. A noisy house on a Saturday afternoon, the whole family talking over each other while one person stands in the kitchen, rolling each ball of meat and frying them to rich, salty perfection.

With crunchy chips, a creamy tomato sauce that packs a little heat and cold feta, this is a bumper recipe. I serve mine as a platter for sharing, but you can easily halve or quarter the quantities. Or why not make a big batch and freeze it?

SERVES 8

For the kjufte

500g (1lb 2oz) pork mince (ground pork)

500g (1lb 2oz) beef mince (ground beef), at least 12% fat

1 medium onion, finely chopped

150g (5½oz) fine breadcrumbs

2 eggs

3 garlic cloves, finely chopped

1½ tsp Vegeta seasoning

1 tsp baking powder

150ml (5fl oz) vegetable oil

50g (1¾oz) plain (all-purpose) flour

Freshly ground black pepper

For the spicy tomato sos

1 tsp olive oil

100g (3½oz) tomato purée (paste)

4 garlic cloves, finely chopped

50g (1¾oz) plain (all-purpose) flour

1 tsp dried chilli flakes

For the chips (fries)

1kg (2¼lb) Cyprus or Maris Piper potatoes

400ml (14fl oz) vegetable oil, for frying

Salt

Dried oregano, to season

To serve

200g (7oz) feta

Gherkins, jalapeños, pickled onions or pickled peppers

The night before serving, place the pork and beef mince, onion, breadcrumbs, eggs, garlic, Vegeta seasoning, and baking powder in a large bowl. Season with black pepper and mix with your hands for a couple of minutes to break up the mince and combine the ingredients. Cover and chill in the fridge overnight.

To make the sauce, heat the oil in a large wide saucepan over a medium heat. Add the tomato purée and cook for about 3 minutes, stirring. Reduce the heat to medium-low, add the garlic and cook for a further minute. Whisk in the flour, a teaspoon at a time, until incorporated to form a very stiff paste. Gradually add 400ml (14fl oz) cold water, whisking after each addition, to form a thick, creamy sauce. Stir in the chilli flakes and season well. Set aside.

To make the chips, slice the potatoes into 1cm (½in) thick chips (fries) and pat dry with kitchen paper (paper towel). Pour the oil into a deep saucepan over a medium-low heat and heat until a small chunk of bread dropped into the oil browns within 8 seconds. Fry the chips in batches for 10 minutes, then set aside to drain on kitchen paper. Retain the oil in the pan and set aside.

To make the kjufte, remove the meat mixture from the fridge, weigh the mixture and divide it into about 24 balls. Pinch each ball in the palm of your hand to bring the mixture together, then roll into an oblong shape, patting each side flat as you go.

Heat the oil for the kjufte in the wide saucepan over a medium heat. Tip the flour into a wide, shallow bowl and gently roll each kjufte in it until lightly coated, shaking off any excess. Fry in batches for 8 minutes per batch or until crispy, taking care not to overcrowd the pan. Remove using a slotted spoon.

Return the pan containing the chip oil to a high heat. Fry the chips for a further 3 minutes or until crispy, then drain on kitchen paper. Transfer to a bowl and season with salt and oregano.

Reheat the tomato sauce over a low heat, whisking until warmed through. Pour half of the sauce onto a large serving platter, smoothing it out with a spatula. Arrange half of the chips on top, then crumble over half of the feta. Repeat with the remaining chips and feta. Arrange the kjufte on top along with dollops of tomato sauce and the pickles.

Photographed on pages 156–157.

Aubergine Kjufte, Lekja, Kebab Shop Garlic Sauce, and Pickled Onions

You can make this kjufte and serve with the sides from page 154, or go for this textural sensation, topped off with a decent version of your favourite kebab shop sauce. I like to use Thomy or any Polish mayo you can find in most big supermarkets.

SERVES 4

Pickled red onion (made by adding 2 thinly sliced red onions to the pickling liquid on page 36)

For the garlic sauce
5 tbsp mayonnaise

5 tbsp full-fat plain yogurt

½ garlic clove

2 tbsp lemon juice

1 tbsp olive oil

Salt, to taste

For the kjufte
Vegetable or sunflower oil, for frying

2 leeks, washed thoroughly and roughly chopped

1 large aubergine (eggplant), roughly chopped

2 garlic cloves, finely chopped

1 bunch of dill, finely chopped

1 egg

120g (4¼oz) panko breadcrumbs

Juice of 1 lemon

Salt and freshly ground black pepper

For the lekja
Vegetable or sunflower oil, for frying

2 onions, finely diced

2 garlic cloves, finely diced

1 tbsp cumin

250g (9oz) green lentils

Two days before serving, prepare the pickled red onion following the recipe on page 36.

To make the garlic sauce, blend all the ingredients together in a blender or food processor. Season with salt to taste and refrigerate until you're ready to serve.

To make the kjufte, heat a little oil in a medium pan over a medium heat. Add the leek and fry for 5–8 minutes or until softened, then add the aubergine and continue to cook for 10–15 minutes or until softened. Transfer to a large bowl and set aside to cool.

Add the garlic, dill, egg, breadcrumbs, and lemon juice to the bowl. Season and mix thoroughly until the mixture comes together. Set aside.

To make the lekja, heat a little oil in a large saucepan over a medium heat. Add the onion and cook for 5 minutes or until softened and translucent. Add the garlic and cumin and continue to cook, stirring, for a couple of minutes.

Add the lentils and stir to completely coat them in the onion and spices. Add 420ml (14¼fl oz) water and bring to the boil. Reduce the heat to low and cook for 30–35 minutes, stirring occasionally, until the lentils are cooked but not falling apart.

To fry the kjufte, pour 7.5cm (3in) oil into a large saucepan over a medium-low heat. Shape each kjufte as in the photograph on pages 156–157 – each one should weigh about 50g (1¾oz). Fry in batches for about 4–5 minutes, or until crispy on the outside.

Pile the kjufte, lekja, garlic sauce, and pickled red onions into serving bowls and allow everyone to help themselves.

Sarma with Smoked Pork Ribs

Mention sarma (pronounced "sarmaah") to anyone from South-Eastern Europe and watch their face melt as they fall into a daydream of stuffed pickled cabbage rolls. The dish is so familiar that it's no wonder the merest hint can evoke such a rush of memories for so many. It's part of a bigger family of foods known as dolma, and you can find another variation on page 138.

It's worth trying to find pickled cabbage for this. You can find whole pickled cabbages or the leaves in jars in most Eastern European or Turkish stores during autumn and winter, or online from magazaonline.co.uk. The same goes for the smoked pork ribs. You can easily replace the minced meat with cooked mushrooms and omit the ribs to make this dish vegan. You can also replace the pork with an equal quantity of beef if you prefer. Sarma are always best made the day before and reheated just before serving, and they freeze really well.

MAKES 12–14

1 whole pickled cabbage or 1.5kg (3lb 3oz) jarred pickled cabbage leaves

Vegetable or sunflower oil, for frying

1 large onion, finely chopped

3 tbsp sweet paprika

10 garlic cloves, finely chopped

250g (9oz) pork mince (ground pork)

250g (9oz) beef mince (ground beef)

200g (7oz) risotto rice

Handful of parsley, roughly chopped

500g (1lb 2oz) smoked pork ribs, separated, or smoked pancetta

7 bay leaves

1 tbsp plain (all-purpose) flour

Salt and freshly ground black pepper

Photographed on page 162.

If you use a whole head of pickled cabbage, carefully peel away each leaf, ensuring the leaves stay as intact as possible.

Using the tip of a knife, shave off the tough, bitter stalk at the bottom of each leaf and discard. Wash each leaf under cold running water to remove excess salt. Set aside any large leaves with holes (usually the first few leaves on the outside of the cabbage) to cover the top of the rolls.

Select 12–14 leaves; you want to make sure that your rolls are going to be similar in size so you may need to overlap 2 smaller-sized leaves to make one larger one. Chop any unused leaves, ensuring the larger leaves you've set aside for the top remain whole, and set aside.

Preheat the oven to 160°C (140°C fan/325°F/Gas 3) and heat a little oil in a frying pan over a medium heat. Once the oil is hot, add the chopped onion and stir until soft and translucent. Add a splash of water followed by 2 tbsp of the smoked paprika and the chopped garlic and cook for a further 2 minutes.

Add the pork and beef mince to the pan to brown, using a fork or potato masher to gently break up any lumps as you go. Add plenty of cracked black pepper and a pinch of salt but be careful to not over season the meat as both the cabbage and pork are salty.

Pour the rice into the pan, add the parsley and stir to combine and coat the rice in the juices (you aren't cooking the rice at this stage). Set aside to cool.

Spoon 60–70g (2–2¼oz) of the cooled filling mixture onto the bottom of a cabbage leaf. Fold each side of the leaf into the centre, then fold the leaf up from the bottom. Gently roll the leaf so it's tightly rolled, but not so tight that it could burst. Fold in the bottom of the leaf and push inwards with your index finger so the whole roll is secured. Repeat for each cabbage leaf until all the filling has been used.

Oil the bottom of a large casserole dish or deep baking tray and add half of the chopped cabbage leaves. Position the sarma evenly over the chopped cabbage, nestling the pork ribs or pancetta in between. Depending on how wide your dish or tray is, you may end up with a couple of layers. Arrange the rest of the chopped cabbage leaves on top, followed by the bay leaves and the large cabbage leaves you set aside earlier.

Pour water into the pan or tray until everything is submerged and cover with a lid or oven-proof plate small enough to fit inside the dish or tray, in case any rolls try to burst open. Cook in the oven for 5 hours, checking regularly and adding more water as necessary to ensure the sarma stay submerged.

Towards the end of the cooking time, put the flour into a small saucepan over a low heat and slowly add 50ml (1¾fl oz) water and the remaining tablespoon of paprika, whisking continuously to form a smooth, thin paste.

Remove the casserole dish or baking tray from the oven and increase the temperature to 200°C (180°C fan/400°F/Gas 6). Remove the large leaves from the top of the sarma and pour over the paprika mixture to cover evenly. Return the dish or tray to the oven for a further 30 minutes or until the top is crunchy, then serve.

Hot Kebapcinja

with Chilli and Honey Relish

Traditionally served with Kajmak (see page 51) and Lepinja (see page 82), raw onion and dried chilli flakes, kebapcinja (pronounced "kebapchinya") is eaten across southeast Europe with only slight variations. If you happen to find yourself in North Macedonia, head to Destan in Skopje for the best. Don't expect frills, take it for what it is – a symbol of how we express ourselves through food, with a note of understated excellence.

The traditional recipe for kebapci is a celebration of simplicity, and this version will be adored by those who like their meals spicy. To serve, arrange all the components on the table and let each person take charge of their own stuffing. For a vegetarian version, replace the mince with crumbled tofu or your favourite meat alternative.

Try to get the meat from a local butcher and ask them to mince it twice, as you want the texture to be smooth and soft. You can swap out the lamb or beef for pork, but using a combination of two different meats is the key to succulence. The kebapcinja will taste even better if you can cook them on a barbecue.

Photographed on page 163.

SERVES 4

For the kebapci

500g (1lb 2oz) lamb mince
  (ground lamb)

500g (1lb 2oz) beef mince
  (ground beef)

1 medium onion, finely grated

3 garlic cloves, finely chopped

2 tsp Vegeta seasoning or salt

1 tsp sweet paprika

1 tsp baking powder

50ml (1¾fl oz) sparkling water

1 egg

2 tbsp smoked paprika

1 tsp chilli flakes

For the relish

1 medium onion, roughly chopped,
  plus extra to serve

2 garlic cloves, roughly chopped

6 green chillies, roughly chopped

150ml (5fl oz) runny honey

100g (3½oz) full-fat plain yogurt

Bunch of parsley

Salt and freshly ground black pepper

For the lepinja

4 Lepinja (see page 82)

Vegetable or sunflower oil, for frying

Olive oil, for drizzling

To serve

300ml (10fl oz) soured cream

Thinly sliced onion

Handful of fresh herbs, such as
  Thai basil, mint, and dill

To make the kebapci, thoroughly combine all the ingredients in a bowl. Cover and refrigerate overnight (this will ensure the meat has a fluffy texture, which is what makes kebapcinja so special).

Meanwhile, make the relish. Add the onion, garlic, chillies, honey, yogurt, and parsley to a blender or food processor and pulse until finely chopped and well combined. Season to taste and set aside in the fridge.

The following day, divide the kebapci mixture into 12 balls and roll each ball into a thin sausage shape (remember they will shrink as they cook) about 2.5cm (1in) thick and as straight as you can make them. Many restaurants use sausage makers to give their kebapcinja a uniformed shape. If you want to be exact, use a piping bag.

Heat the grill (broiler) to high and place the kebapcinja onto a lightly oiled baking sheet. Grill for 10–12 minutes or until cooked all the way through but still soft and bouncy in the centre.

If needed, reheat the lepinja. Heat a little oil in a frying pan over a medium heat. Add the lepinja and fry for about 1 minute on each side. Drizzle with olive oil.

Serve the kebapci, lepinja, and relish with the soured cream, thinly sliced onion, and fresh herbs.

Slow Cooked Harissa Lamb with Sweet Peaches, Urda, and Herbs

We are definitely not afraid of heat in the Balkans, but it's usually in the form of a raw or pickled hot pepper served on the side of a dish, or a raw white or spring onion – straightforward ways to bring a little heat to the meal.

Aromatic spices are more unusual. The fruitiness that the harissa brings to this lamb dish not only complements the sweetness, but brings a whole new dimension to a dish that is familiar to many. The leftovers taste really good squeezed into wrap.

SERVES 6

For the peaches

200g (7oz) caster (superfine) sugar

Juice of 1 lemon

3 peaches, stoned and halved

For the lamb

2.25kg (5lb) leg of lamb

100g (3½oz) harissa (80g/2¾oz if using Lamiri harissa)

2 cloves of garlic, roughly chopped, plus 2 heads of garlic, halved, skin on

1 bunch of thyme

50ml (1¾fl oz) vegetable oil

Juice of 1 lemon

2 tsp salt

1 tbsp freshly ground black pepper

5 carrots, halved lengthways

3 medium onions, halved

4 bay leaves

1 lamb stock cube dissolved in 600ml (1 pint) hot water

200ml (7fl oz) red wine

To serve

100g (3½oz) Urda (see page 52) or ricotta

Oregano, mint or basil

Three days before serving, prepare the peaches. Add 600ml (1 pint) water, the sugar, and lemon juice to a medium saucepan over a medium heat. Bring to the boil and boil for 10 minutes or until the mixture forms a runny syrup. Set aside to cool.

Transfer the cooled syrup to a jar or airtight container. Submerge the peaches in the syrup, cover and set aside in the fridge for at least 3 days.

The day before serving, marinate the leg of lamb by rubbing the harissa, chopped garlic, and thyme all over the flesh with the vegetable oil, lemon juice, salt, and pepper. Wrap tightly in cling film (plastic wrap) and leave in the fridge overnight.

Remove the lamb from the fridge 30 minutes before cooking. Preheat the oven to 200°C (180°Cfan/400°F/Gas 6).

Transfer the lamb to a large, deep, well-oiled baking tray. Arrange the carrots, onions, 2 heads of garlic, and bay leaves around the lamb and pour over the stock and red wine. Cook for 15 minutes or until just beginning to brown.

Remove the lamb from the oven and reduce the oven temperature to 140°C (120°C fan/275°F/Gas 1).

Cover the baking tray with foil and cook for 6–7 hours or until the meat falls away from the bone (the exact cooking time will depend on the weight of the leg), basting the meat with its juices every 30 minutes or so. Remove the foil for the final 15 minutes of cooking time.

Meanwhile, remove the preserved peaches from the fridge at least 1 hour before serving.

Allow the lamb to rest for 10 minutes, then transfer the lamb and vegetables to a serving plate. Garnish with the preserved peaches, urda, and herbs.

Photographed on pages 168–169.

Oris Tava

The word tava literally translates to pan, and oris means rice, so oris tava is a baked rice dish. This much-loved midweek meal can be made with or without meat but is most commonly a dish of baked chicken with rice. It's traditionally made with peas and carrots but you can also substitute the vegetables with any of your choosing, as I have.

SERVES 6

6 chicken thighs, skin on

Olive oil, for drizzling

Juice of 1 lemon

4 tbsp butter at room temperature, plus extra for greasing

2 onions, roughly chopped

2 aubergines (eggplant) cut into 5cm (2in) chunks

4 garlic cloves, roughly chopped

400g (14oz) long-grain rice

2 tbsp Vegeta seasoning

1 tsp ground turmeric

1 bunch of tarragon, leaves picked, or 4 tbsp dried tarragon – reserve some for garnishing

4 plums, green or regular, stoned and halved

Runny honey, to drizzle

Salt and freshly ground black pepper

Place the chicken thighs in a large baking tray. Drizzle with olive oil and the lemon juice and season with salt and pepper. Cover and refrigerate for 4 hours.

Twenty minutes before cooking, remove the chicken from the fridge. Preheat the oven to 180°C (160°C fan/350°F/Gas 4).

Melt the butter in a large saucepan over a medium heat and add the onions. Fry for 5 minutes or until softened, stirring frequently to prevent them catching.

Add the aubergines and garlic, and cook for a further 5 minutes.

Add the rice, Vegeta, turmeric, tarragon, and seasoning and stir to combine and coat the rice. Transfer to a well-greased baking tray, spread out evenly and pour over 800ml (1½ pints) water.

Arrange the chicken in the tray, skin-side up, and bake in the oven for 45 minutes.

Arrange the plums around the chicken and cook for a further 15 minutes or until the rice is cooked, the chicken skin is crispy, and the plums are golden. Drizzle honey over the plums and sprinkle the reserved tarragon over the rice and chicken.

Podvarok

This baked sausage and sauerkraut dish (pronounced "pod-va-rak") epitomizes the beauty of this humble vegetable. As with Sarma (see page 160), if striving for authenticity it really should be baked in a large clay pot. This easy dish is traditionally made with smoked meat for special occasions, and here I add hot chunks of salami to cover the vegetables in a sea of savoury flavours. However, it can be made vegetarian or vegan by substituting the meat for vegetables. It's traditionally made by chopping a whole, pickled cabbage, but I used sauerkraut for ease.

Drain the sauerkraut into a sieve and rinse with cold water to remove excess salt. Set aside.

Melt the butter in a medium saucepan over a medium heat. Add the onions and cook for 5 minutes or until softened. Add the paprika, Vegeta, and garlic and season with black pepper. Stir to combine and cook for a further 5 minutes. Preheat the oven to 160°C (140°C fan/325°F/Gas 3).

Add the sauerkraut and bay leaves to the pan and mix thoroughly. Transfer to a well-oiled baking tray and spread out evenly. Top with the salami and cook for 1 hour.

SERVES 6

900g (2lb) sauerkraut with carrots

50g (1¾oz) butter

2 onions, finely diced

1 tbsp smoked paprika

1 tbsp Vegeta seasoning or
  1 vegetable stock cube

5 garlic cloves, finely diced

10 bay leaves

700g (1½lb) salami, roughly chopped

Freshly ground black pepper

Kompir Mandza

This vegan potato stew (pronounced "kompeer manje") is hugely popular in North Macedonia, both during lent and outside of it. It's served hot in winter and lukewarm in summer.

I often hear that it's hard to find good meatless dishes in the Balkans, but this is definitely not the case. As a region that heavily practises traditions of Orthodox Christianity, the ancient calendar still governs so much of how we eat, and that includes the 46 days of lent when no animal products are consumed.

I serve this with salsa verde and some crusty bread to dip in the garlic-heavy sauce and, of course, to mop up all the delicious juices at the end.

SERVES 6

For the stew

200ml (7fl oz) vegetable oil

3 white onions, finely sliced

2 tbsp paprika

7 garlic cloves, finely chopped

2 carrots, finely chopped

1kg (2¼lb) potatoes, peeled and chopped into 9-cm (3½-in) chunks

1 tbsp Vegeta seasoning or 1 stock cube

4 bay leaves

Handful of parsley, chopped

Salt and freshly ground black pepper

For the salsa verde

Bunch of dill

Bunch of mint

Bunch of parsley

Bunch of basil

50g (1¾oz) capers

2 garlic cloves

5 tbsp olive oil

Zest and juice of 1 lemon

To make the stew, heat the oil in a large saucepan over a low heat and add the onions. Cook very slowly, stirring frequently, until softened and translucent.

Add the paprika and 100ml (3½fl oz) water and cook for a further 5 minutes, stirring continuously.

Add the garlic and carrots and stir to combine. Add the potatoes, 700ml (1¼ pints) water, the Vegeta seasoning or stock cube, and bay leaves and bring to the boil. Simmer for 25–30 minutes or until the potatoes are cooked but not falling apart and season to taste. The stew can be stored for up to 4 days in the fridge in a sealed container and freezes well.

To make the salsa verde, simply add all the ingredients to a blender or food processor and blitz until smooth.

Serve with the parsley and a big dollop of salsa verde on top, and some crusty bread on the side. Any unused salsa verde can be stored for up to 7 days in the fridge in a sealed container.

Turli Tava

Turli (pronounced "toorli") means mixed in Turkish, and this dish is a big mish mash of baked vegetables that is so easy to prepare and best made on a Sunday or at the beginning of the week, to prepare for the whirlwind days ahead. There are many variations, but the best part is always mopping up the oil with chunks of bread.

You can use any vegetables you like but bear in mind that cooking times will vary. If you're using okra be sure not to add it any earlier or it will turn to mush.

SERVES 4

4 large tomatoes, roughly chopped into large chunks

1 large aubergine (eggplant), roughly chopped into large chunks

2 red onions, roughly chopped into large chunks

1 large carrot, roughly chopped into large chunks

1 large potato, roughly chopped into large chunks

1 green (bell) pepper, roughly chopped into large chunks

1 red (bell) pepper, roughly chopped into large chunks

6 garlic cloves, roughly chopped

3 tbsp paprika

3 tbsp Vegeta seasoning

7 bay leaves

150ml (5fl oz) olive oil, plus extra for oiling

15 okra

4 corn on the cob

1 tsp chilli flakes

Juice of 1 lemon

Salt and freshly ground black pepper

Preheat the oven to 170°C (150°C fan/325°F/Gas 3). Place all the vegetables except for the okra and corn into a large well-oiled baking tray and season.

Add the paprika, Vegeta and bay leaves and stir to combine. Pour over the olive oil and cook for 1½ hours.

Remove from the oven and add the okra and corn on the cob. Return to the oven for a further 15 minutes.

To serve, season the corn on the cob lightly with salt and the chilli flakes and squeeze the lemon juice all over to lift the richness of the oil. Serve with chunks of bread.

Yufki

These egg noodles are usually made in the dead heat of late August so they can be dried out in the sun and so that the dough melts as you roll. I have visions of them hanging over chairs and tables, the smell of clean linen... the sight of the noodles drying out is magical. The dried noodles are bagged up into cotton sacks ready for that special yufki moment that might grab you in the middle of the night or morning. I was lucky enough to make a batch of yufki (pronounced "yoofky") with Valentina on her farm just outside Skopje. Valentina makes yufki at the speed of light, a skill she developed after moving to a farm and finding herself with an abundance of eggs. Making noodles was the obvious solution, and now she bags up and sells her yufki to a small selection of customers, delivering them on her bike.

I've still got a small bag of my nan's yufki stored at the back of a kitchen cupboard, as I've never been fully able to let go of the memory of her making them for me no matter the time of night, or morning. She'd pretend she wasn't hungry to begin with but would always join me with a big chunk of cheese in her hand.

Don't be tempted to refrigerate the dried noodles as they'll end up soggy, and you can always use a pasta machine here if you have one. You will need half a quantity of fresh yufki sheets for the lasagne on page 179, and the remainder can be dried and stored for future use. Use the yufki as you would any other kind of pasta.

SERVES 10

6 eggs
100ml (3½fl oz) full-fat (whole) milk
720g (1lb 9oz) plain (all-purpose) flour, sifted
1 tbsp salt
Vegetable oil, for drizzling

To serve
Butter or olive oil
Brined white cheese or feta

Add all the ingredients, except for the oil, to a large bowl. Mix to combine and bring the dough together with your hands.

Turn the dough out onto a lightly floured surface and knead for 10 minutes. Transfer to a well-oiled bowl and cover the top of the dough with oil. Cover the dough (not the bowl) with cling film (plastic wrap) and leave in a warm place for 1 hour.

Turn the dough out onto a lightly floured surface once more and knead for a further 10 minutes.

Divide the dough into 12 balls and roll each ball out as thinly as you can, the thinner the better!

You can now either cut the dough into thin noodles or leave the pieces whole. If you're making the lasagne on page 179, set aside 6 of the whole dough pieces now.

To dry the yufki, hanging the noodles over a clothes rail with several tiers works well (that's my technique in my London flat), or over the backs of chairs or on clean linens, if you have the space. Leave to dry for 12–24 hours; the warmer it is the quicker they will dry.

To cook the dried yufki, bring a well-oiled saucepan of boiling water to the boil. Add the yufki and cook while stirring (as they easily stick) for 10 minutes or until soft.

Serve with melted butter or oil and plenty of cheese.

Green Goddess Yufki Lasagne

I found such affinity with Valentina when we made yufki together (see page 176) and enjoyed my time perched on her sofa eating her infamous pork, yufki lasagne, and homemade cheeses with a giant pickle on the side. This no-fuss, circular way of eating sparked something in me. I make this lasagne as a ceremonial way to mark the latest batch of yufki, but you can also use pre-made lasagne sheets if you're pushed for time.

SERVES 6

Bunch of parsley

Bunch of dill

Bunch of basil

Bunch of tarragon, leaves picked, or 3 tbsp dried tarragon

150g (5½oz) pine nuts

100g (3½oz) walnuts

50ml (1¾fl oz) olive oil, plus extra for frying

600g (1lb 5oz) mild pickled peppers, such as lombardi

300g (10oz) ricotta

1 garlic clove

2 eggs

1kg (2¼lb) leeks, cleaned and very finely sliced

300ml (10fl oz) double (heavy) cream

½ quantity fresh yufki sheets (see page 176)

200g (7oz) Parmesan, grated, plus extra to serve

Salt and freshly ground black pepper

Olive oil or truffle oil, to serve

Add the herbs, pine nuts, walnuts, and olive oil to a blender or food processor. Blend until smooth and set aside.

Add the pickled peppers to the clean blender or food processor. Blend until smooth and set aside.

Add the ricotta and garlic to the clean blender or food processor. Blend until smooth, season and add the eggs. Stir to combine and set aside.

Heat a little olive oil in a large saucepan over a medium heat. Add the leeks and fry for 5–8 minutes or until softened. Add the herb and pine nut mixture and the cream and continue to cook, stirring, for 15 minutes. Set aside.

Preheat the oven to 180°C (160°C fan/350°F/Gas 4). Cut the yufki to the size of the baking tray you will be using if necessary.

Place a sheet of yufki into the bottom of a well-oiled deep medium baking tray. Covering with some of the leek mixture and a healthy sprinkle of Parmesan. You're going to end up with about 6 layers.

Repeat with the remaining yufki and leek mixture. Top the final leek layer with a fresh yufki sheet. Top this with the pickled peppers followed by the ricotta mixture. Sprinkle with Parmesan and cook for 40 minutes or until the top is crispy.

Allow the lasagne to cool slightly before serving covered in Parmesan and drizzled with a little olive or truffle oil.

Fried Chicken, Kaçamak, and Green Tomato Hot Sauce

Kaçamak (pronounced "kach-a-mak") is a savoury, porridge-like dish made from cornmeal and eaten in Western Asia and areas of South-Eastern Europe. It was originally a low-cost dish eaten by the poor but has now entered the realm of timeless Balkan recipes. Each country in these regions has their own way of making it – some add potatoes, others use pork scratchings, kajmak, grape molasses, bacon, meat cooked in butter, or cheese – but it's so good with whatever you want to put on it.

Here I've made the dish even more satisfying and comforting by adding soft cheese and crunchy fried chicken, but you can go ahead and try topping it with whatever you fancy – it's very easy to make it vegetarian, too. It's lovely served alongside Zelena Salata (see page 108).

SERVES 4

For the brine

4–8 skinless boneless chicken thighs (depending on size)

300ml (10fl oz) full-fat (whole) milk

300ml (10fl oz) full-fat plain yogurt

5 garlic cloves, roughly chopped

2 tsp ground turmeric

3 tbsp white wine vinegar

1 tbsp salt

1 tbsp ground pepper

For the coating

150g (5½oz) plain (all-purpose) flour

1 tsp baking powder

2 tbsp garlic powder

1 tbsp smoked paprika

50g (1¾oz) cornflour (cornstarch)

1 tbsp ground pepper

1 tbsp salt

5 eggs, whisked

About 400ml (14fl oz) vegetable oil, or enough to cover the chicken

For the kaçamak

100ml (3½fl oz) full-fat (whole) milk

2 tsp salt

125g (4½oz) cornmeal

Salt and freshly ground black pepper

To serve

70g (2½oz) butter

1 tbsp smoked paprika

150g (5½oz) feta or canned creamy white cheese (from Turkish or Eastern European stores)

Green Tomato Hot Sauce (see page 28)

Ideally brine the chicken 24 hours in advance but if you're in a hurry, a minimum of 4 hours will do. Place the chicken into a large container with a lid. Combine the remaining brine ingredients and pour over the chicken, ensuring the chicken is well coated. Cover and set aside in the fridge.

To make the crunchy coating, thoroughly mix all the dry ingredients together and place in a large bowl or in a deep tray large enough to hold the chicken pieces. Set aside.

To make the kaçamak, pour the milk and 600ml (1 pint) water into a large saucepan over a high heat and add the salt. Bring to the boil and reduce the heat to medium. Slowly pour in the cornmeal, stirring constantly, and continue to stir for around 10 minutes.

The kaçamak can be made ahead of time. To reheat, add a splash of milk and whisk well over a medium heat until the original consistency is reached.

Towards the end of the brining time, place the egg into a shallow container and season. Heat the oil in a large saucepan over a medium heat.

Remove the chicken from the brine. Dip the chicken in the flour coating, then the whisked egg, then back in the flour, ensuring the chicken is well coated.

Test the temperature of the oil by dropping in a small piece of battered chicken. If it's ready, the chicken will turn a nice, even golden brown. You don't want the oil to be too hot, as the batter will become too dark too quickly and the chicken won't cook evenly.

Drop the chicken into the hot oil and cook for around 10 minutes, turning once very carefully to prevent the coating coming away from the chicken, or until cooked all the way through (test by inserting a skewer into the meat at the widest point and checking the juices run clear). Don't overcrowd the pan and work in batches as needed. Drain on kitchen paper (paper towel).

To serve, melt the butter in a small saucepan over a low heat and whisk in the paprika. Remove from the heat. Spoon the kaçamak into individual serving bowls and pour over the butter. Top with crumbled feta or white cheese, the fried chicken and lashings of Green Tomato Hot Sauce (see page 28).

Photographed on page 182.

Hot Ajvar Sausage Bake
with Garlic Greens and Mozzarella

A really simple recipe that, as with anything deep and saucy, is even better the next day. This should be your gateway to using ajvar in any tomato sauce; add it to bolognese or soup and make it your everyday go-to ingredient. Either use the recipe on page 27 or substitute for a store-bought version. There are lots of ajvar imitations out there so try to buy from Macedonian producers if possible, of which there are many – I recommend the Mamma's brand. Serve with bread to mop up the juices or potatoes to absorb every flavour.

SERVES 3–4

Olive oil, for frying

2 medium onions, finely chopped

2 garlic cloves, finely chopped

400g (14oz) can chopped tomatoes

2 tbsp caster (superfine) sugar

400g (14oz) spring greens,
    finely shredded

3 tbsp garlic powder

1 preserved lemon, finely chopped

6 sausages (British-style bangers
    work nicely)

250g (9oz) ajvar (shop-bought
    or see page 27)

450g (1lb) mozzarella, torn

30g (1oz) breadcrumbs

Salt and freshly ground black pepper

Photographed on page 183.

Heat a splash of oil in a medium frying pan over a medium heat and cook the onions for 5 minutes or until softened, stirring often. Add the garlic and continue to cook, stirring, for a further 5 minutes or until softened.

Add the tomatoes, fill the can with water and pour this into the pan. Add the sugar, season with salt and stir to combine. Reduce the heat to low and cook for 15 minutes. Set aside.

Preheat the oven to 170°C (150°C fan/325°F/Gas 3). Add a splash of oil to a large saucepan over a medium heat and add the spring greens and 100ml (3½fl oz) water. Cook, stirring continuously, for 10 minutes or until the greens start to break down.

Add the garlic powder and preserved lemon and continue to cook for 15–20 minutes or until completely softened.

Heat a large frying pan over a medium heat and fry the sausages until just browned all over.

Pour the tomato sauce, spring greens and ajvar into a well-oiled large baking tray and mix thoroughly. Arrange the sausages in the tray (pour in any juice from the pan) and bake in the oven for 15 minutes.

Stir the sauce to prevent the top from browning too much, then return to the oven for 10 minutes.

Top with the mozzarella, then sprinkle over the breadcrumbs and season lightly. Return to the oven for 10 minutes or until the cheese has melted and the breadcrumbs are golden.

Rebra u Kajmak

An old-school Serbian recipe of beef ribs in kajmak (a thick salted cream, see page 51) that was probably developed to tenderize tougher cuts of meat. It's a surprising combination that deserves a giant pile of fluffy mashed potatoes.

You can use any kind of rib, and if you don't have the time to make kajmak, clotted cream can be used as an alternative. Just don't be tempted to add the kajmak in any sooner or it will split.

SERVES 6

1.5kg (3lb 3oz) beef ribs, separated

Vegetable oil, for frying

6 shallots, halved

1 leek, washed and cut into large chunks

5 garlic cloves, halved

Bunch of rosemary

1 beef stock cube dissolved in 300ml (10fl oz) hot water

500g (1lb 2oz) new potatoes

250g (9oz) Kajmak (see page 51) or clotted cream

Salt and freshly ground black pepper

Preheat the oven to 160°C (140°C fan/325°F/Gas 3). Season the ribs and rub the seasoning in well. Heat a little oil in a large frying pan over a medium heat and fry the ribs on all sides until browned. Set aside.

Arrange the ribs in a large, well-oiled baking tray and add the shallots, leek, garlic, and rosemary. Pour the stock over, cover with foil and roast for 3½ hours, basting the meat with the liquid from the dish every hour or so.

Remove the dish from the oven, add the potatoes and dollops of kajmak, and return to the oven, uncovered, for 40 minutes. Serve with fluffy mashed potatoes.

Mascarpone Croquettes
and Mish Mash

"Mish mash" is an extremely technical term for a light summer dish, usually made in both North Macedonia and Bulgaria, consisting of tomatoes, peppers, egg, and sometimes cheese. I love the name almost as much as another very formal saying: "chat pat", which roughly translates to "sometimes" or "here and there". Mish mash is quick and easy to make and essential for some deep summer frying. You can eat it on its own as a toast topper or pair it with these creamy and tangy croquettes for a more filling meal.

SERVES 4–5

For the croquettes

450g (1lb) Maris Piper potatoes (or other floury variety), roughly chopped

200g (7oz) mascarpone

80g (2¾oz) tapenade or blended green olives

Large bunch of basil, roughly chopped, plus 6 whole leaves to garnish

2 garlic cloves, finely chopped

1 tbsp white wine vinegar

3 eggs

400ml (14fl oz) vegetable oil

50g (1¾oz) plain (all-purpose) flour

100g (3½oz) fine breadcrumbs

Salt and freshly ground black pepper

For the mish mash

3 long green peppers

3 long red peppers

4 medium tomatoes

Olive oil, for frying

1 onion, roughly chopped

3 garlic cloves, roughly chopped

1 tsp caster (superfine) sugar

4 eggs

100g (3½oz) brined white cheese or feta, broken into chunks

Salt and freshly ground black pepper

To serve

Olive oil

Olives

6 basil leaves

To make the croquettes, the day before serving add the potatoes to a large saucepan of salted water over a medium heat. Bring to the boil and cook for 10–15 minutes or until soft. Drain and set aside to cool.

Transfer the potatoes to a large bowl and mash until smooth. Add the mascarpone, tapenade, basil, garlic, vinegar, and 2 of the eggs. Mix thoroughly to combine. Cover and refrigerate overnight (this mixture also makes great vegetarian burgers).

To make the mish mash, preheat the grill (broiler) to high and grill the peppers and tomatoes for 10 minutes, or until the skins are just softened, turning after 5 minutes. Transfer to a bowl and cover with cling film (plastic wrap) or to an airtight container and set aside for 15 minutes.

Carefully peel away the skins but don't worry about the seeds – I always think they add extra flavour to this dish. Roughly chop and set aside.

Heat a little olive oil in a medium non-stick frying pan over a medium heat. Add the onion and fry for 5 minutes or until soft.

Add the garlic, peppers, tomatoes, and sugar and cook, stirring, for a further 15 minutes.

Add the eggs and cheese and continue to cook, stirring, for 5 minutes. Season to taste and set aside to cool.

To cook the croquettes, heat the vegetable oil in a large saucepan over a medium heat for 8 minutes. Meanwhile place the flour, remaining egg, and breadcrumbs into separate bowls and season.

Roll the croquette mixture into 10 spheres each weighing about 50g (1¾oz). Dip each croquette first in the flour, then egg, and finally the breadcrumbs.

Fry the croquettes in batches, carefully moving them around in the oil and taking care not to overcrowd the pan, for about 4 minutes or until crispy and golden brown. Drain on kitchen paper (paper towel).

Transfer the mish mash to a serving plate, top with the croquettes and drizzle with lashings of olive oil. Garnish with olives and basil leaves.

Creamed Spanak and Cured Egg Yolks

Due to the differing prices between countries, I would always light up when I saw my mum defrosting a big bag of frozen spinach, a sentiment shared by members of different diasporas. My version, with cured egg yolks, is best eaten with a big spoon as a late-summer dinner. It will take about 15 hours to cure the egg yolks; if you want them firmer just leave them for longer.

SERVES 6 AS PART OF A MEAL OR 3 AS A MAIN

For the cured egg yolks
150g (5½oz) salt
150g (5½oz) caster (superfine) sugar
6 egg yolks

For the creamed spanak
2 tbsp sesame oil
2 onions, finely diced
750g (1lb 10oz) frozen spinach, defrosted and drained
180g (6oz) basmati rice
3 tbsp Pickled Wild Garlic Oil (see page 111) or 3 garlic cloves, finely diced
300ml (10fl oz) double (heavy) cream
Salt and freshly ground black pepper

To serve
Chilli sauce
Plain yogurt

To make the cured egg yolks, the day before serving mix the salt and sugar together until well combined. Spread half of the sugar and salt mixture onto the bottom of a baking tray. Make 6 wells in the mixture and carefully place an egg yolk into each well. Cover with the remaining salt and sugar mixture, cover with cling film (plastic wrap) and refrigerate for at least 15 hours (the longer you leave them, the firmer the egg yolks will be).

Rinse the egg yolks in cold water and very gently pat dry with a clean tea towel or kitchen paper (paper towel). Set aside until ready to serve.

Preheat the oven to 180°C (160°C fan/350°F/Gas 4). To make the spanak, heat the sesame oil in a medium saucepan over a medium heat. Add the onions and fry for 5 minutes or until soft.

Add the spinach and continue to cook, stirring, for a further 5 minutes.

Add the rice, wild garlic oil or garlic cloves, and the cream, season well and stir to combine. Remove from the heat.

Transfer the spinach to a well-oiled baking tray and flatten with a spatula. Pour over 400ml (14fl oz) water and bake for 15 minutes.

Remove the tray from the oven, stir thoroughly, and return to the oven for a further 15 minutes or until crispy on top.

To serve, make 6 wells in the spanak and add a cured egg yolk to each well. Serve with plenty of hot chilli sauce and some plain yogurt.

Hot Ribnik

This baked fish dish is traditionally made without chilli, but I like it with. It's an effortless and perfectly healthy meal to add to your weekly rota. You can swap out the fish for your preferred type or leave out the chilli if you're not in the mood.

SERVES 4

Olive oil, for frying and drizzling
5 medium onions, halved
6 garlic cloves, halved
1kg (2¼lb) passata (tomato purée)
1 tbsp caster (superfine) sugar
4 sea bass, cod, or pollock fillets
3 green chillies, finely sliced

Heat a little olive oil in a large saucepan over a medium heat. Add the onions and 100ml (3½fl oz) water and cook, stirring constantly, for 5 minutes or until they begin to change colour (a little bite is crucial).

Add the garlic, passata and sugar and cook for 20–25 minutes.

Meanwhile, if using skin-on fish, heat a little oil in a wide frying pan over a high heat. Season the fish well and fry, skin-side down, for 2 minutes or until it starts to puff up. Don't be tempted to move the fish, as this will break the skin.

Preheat the oven to 180°C (160°C fan/350°F/Gas 4). Transfer the onion mixture to a well-oiled large baking tray and place the fish on top, skin-side up. Bake for 12–14 minutes or until the fish is cooked through but still tender.

Scatter over the chillies, drizzle with olive oil and serve.

The Ultimate Musaka

This ex-Yugo version of musaka isn't made with
béchamel sauce but instead uses eggs and yogurt
to create a firmer, fluffier top. It also doesn't include
the heady sweetness of cinnamon. My favourite
version as a kid was made simply with marrow,
meat, and potatoes, but since then I've explored a
whole universe of musaka, eaten my way through
all the variations, and gathered various recipes, all
leading up to this moment.

SERVES 6

For the aubergines

50g (1¾oz) plain (all-purpose) flour

3 medium aubergines (eggplant),
    cut into 5mm (¼in) slices

100ml (3½fl oz) vegetable oil

For the cheese sauce

Vegetable oil, for frying

3 large leeks (about 350g/12oz),
    roughly sliced

300ml (10fl oz) double (heavy) cream

300g (10oz) ricotta

200g (7oz) grated gruyere

1 tsp chilli flakes

5 garlic cloves, roughly chopped

For the meat sauce

Vegetable oil, for frying

1 large onion, roughly chopped

1 tbsp smoked paprika

800g (1¾lb) lamb mince (ground
    lamb), beef mince (ground beef)
    or pork mince (ground pork), at
    least 20% fat

1 beef, lamb or chicken stock cube

½ bunch of parsley, roughly chopped

To assemble

5 Maris Piper potatoes, very thinly
    sliced

5 eggs

500g (1lb 2oz) full-fat Greek yogurt

100g (3½oz) grated Parmesan

Salt and freshly ground black pepper

Place the flour into a shallow dish and season. Dip the aubergine slices into the flour to coat and set aside for 5 minutes.

Heat the oil in a large saucepan over a medium heat for 8 minutes. Carefully add the aubergine slices and fry in batches for 3–4 minutes, turning once, or until the outside is sealed. Drain on kitchen paper (paper towel) and set aside.

To make the cheese sauce, heat a little oil in a medium saucepan over a low heat. Add the leeks and cook, stirring, for 5 minutes or until they begin to soften.

Add the double cream and stir thoroughly to combine. Gradually add the ricotta and gruyere, stirring well after each addition, until completely melted. Cook on low for 15 minutes, add the chilli flakes and garlic, and set aside.

To make the meat sauce, heat a little oil in a medium saucepan over a medium heat. Add the onion and paprika and cook, stirring, for 5 minutes or until softened.

Add the minced meat and stock cube and cook for 5 minutes, breaking the meat up with a wooden spoon, until browned.

Add the parsley and 50ml (1¾fl oz) water and stir to combine. Cook for a further 8 minutes or until most of the water has evaporated. Season and set aside.

Preheat the oven to 170°C (150°C fan/325°F/Gas 3). Take a large, well-oiled deep baking dish and slice the potatoes as thin as possible.

To assemble the musaka, go wild and create as many layers as you like. Arrange some of the potatoes on the bottom of a well-oiled baking tray to soak up the juices. Spoon some of the meat sauce over the top, followed by a layer of aubergine. Repeat until you've used up all of the potato, meat sauce, and aubergine. Cover with foil or a lid and bake for 1 hour.

Meanwhile whisk the eggs with the yogurt and Parmesan. Season and set aside.

Remove the baking tray from the oven and pour over the cheese sauce, followed by the egg and yogurt mixture. Return to the oven, uncovered, for a further 20 minutes or until the yogurt has set and the potatoes are cooked through.

Allow to cool for 10 minutes before serving with pickled peppers and a green salad.

Photographed on pages 194–195.

Заслад

Indulgent

Desserts

All Roads Lead to Palma

I often wonder if people are open enough about the process you go through as a chef when writing a book. It's like you're pulling something out of you, and hands that are born to cook, with sore palms from rolling dough, switch to typing, constant obsessions, and countless sleepless nights. If the subject has some personal meaning, get ready for a rollercoaster of self-doubt and even an existential crisis. But if you're lucky, like me, it will become all you ever needed to feel at home with your own identity. An opportunity to have a voice, to make it heard – a golden ticket to really explaining yourself, once and for all.

Before I get to the comfortable part, let's start with the doubt. As the idea started to manifest, I wondered if my memories would be sufficient in painting a picture. Did I ask the right questions when I watched my elders cooking? Did I observe their hands enough? Should I have been writing all of this down? Was I even Macedonian enough to do this? Have I ever really been Macedonian enough? Am I too Macedonian to be considered British? These thoughts would drive me wild while I sat sobbing on the floor of my kitchen in Brixton. I just wasn't sure if I could do it. It was in that moment that it hit me just how much I missed it, my other home, having not been back for two and a half years because of the pandemic. So I took all that I had and booked a flight, to remind me of what I was really missing.

When I first got to North Macedonia, all I wanted to do was sleep. I didn't know where to start so I'd close my eyes and nervously wake up every 15 minutes, jolted awake by thunderstorms and remembering why I came here, and the huge task ahead. I'd go through every cupboard for hours on end, staring at crockery, little spoons, looking for inspiration in all the wrong places, wallowing in the idea that I just couldn't get this right. The pressure of honouring my ancestors and the traditions weighing down on me.

While in North Macedonia, I was asked to appear on morning television to talk about Mystic Burek and they asked where I'd feel most comfortable being filmed. I chose Palma, a sweet-tooth institution and Baba Slavka's favourite dessert shop, a name everyone in the city is familiar with not only for their sensational in-house cakes and ice creams but for serving the community for over 50 years.

I popped in and grabbed a glass of water from one of the young wait staff, something to wet my anxiously bitten lips, while nervously weaving in and out of my broken Macedonian. I was feeling totally out of practice, but as it dawned on me what was really happening I started to warm up. I was sitting in my nan's favourite dessert shop, about to be broadcast on a TV show she would have blasted out in the living room. I basked in a sense of pride, not just for this moment but for all that I had achieved.

I returned to the counter, this time in a celebratory mood, pointing to the tulumbi, sour cherry cream cakes, walnut cookies, and more. Piling up my order I added an iced coffee and my eyes glazed over,

that needed filling, something that's always happened to me in moments of extreme emotion, even when I was a kid. I look up and notice the man serving me seemed to be analysing my face, working me out. I wondered if it was my accent he had noticed, but I hoped it was a family resemblance that would make him ask who my grandparents were – a classic Balkan question upon meeting. It turns out that not only did he know them, but he hung out with them, and described my nan as "not just a customer, but a friend". I had to break it to him that neither of them were still around. Just knowing them isn't that unusual as they were a popular pair around these parts. Dedo Mirko (my grandad) was recognisable because he had lost his arms in an accident on the rail tracks when he was younger but still painted using a paintbrush in his mouth, and held a respected position in the government. There is only one picture that exists of us; me as a toddler, just before we lost him to cancer. Baba on the other hand was best known for her cheeky humour, her unbreakable warmth towards all, her obsession with food, and for knowing everyone. The knowledge that the waiter knew who I was just from watching me order sent me rushing outside, desperate to sit down, eat, and cry.

Sitting outside in the hot morning sun I didn't really care what I looked like as I wept, scooping cream off myself as it fell, occasionally laughing manically. Just then, it all started to make

some sense. Not only did I have a legacy to continue but I had to find a way to preserve our way of living, loving, cooking, hosting, and eating with reckless abandon. I want to be remembered for my warmth, just like my Baba, even by the man that works at the dessert shop.

This book has not only been an opportunity to paint a picture of culture, history, and traditions, but also a representation of change. Change can be good; it's definitely inevitable. Migration is change, food adapts to its surroundings, cultures mix, flavours clash, life becomes more diverse and more beautiful.

Not feeling comfortable with who you are can be quite isolating. It's a very specific lack of confidence that comes from lurking in a space of confused identity. I used to feel nervous ordering a beer in Skopje, waiting for someone to laugh at my accent, and feel fear when opening up my lunchbox at school, the very sight of a pickled pepper in my sandwich seemingly screaming "FOREIGNER!" out into the school hallways for all to hear.

Through my own take on second-generation cooking, I've met so many people who are, low and behold, just like me. They grew up with sarma, rakija and Sainsbury's coleslaw on the table at Christmas, *Top of the Pops* on in the living room for the young ones, and turbo folk blasting in the kitchen for the elders. We have our own names for things, squeezy keputch or a bag of crips, and just because an ice cream box is out, don't expect something

sweet – it's probably got some savoury leftovers in it. We want to celebrate the traditions of our ancestors but we also want to time stamp our own journeys through our wide and wonderful diaspora.

Although it was grief that first led me to my business and subsequently this book, this isn't just about Baba; this is about sharing my journey of finding my way back to myself, in the hope that others can connect or learn a little more about being Balkan and being of a third culture.

I'll end on a quote from mum: "You will never truly belong anywhere unless you understand your roots and find your own way to appreciate them."

Orange Ravanija
with Brown Sugar Cream

Ravanija (pronounced "ravaneeya") – also known as ravani in Greece, revani in Turkey, and rawani in Yemen – is a much-adored cake that's served drenched in syrup on its own or with double (heavy) cream or yogurt. It can be made with semolina for a lighter sponge, but I've gone for the heavier version that uses coconut as I love the contrast of the dense, wet cake and sweet, whipped cream.

SERVES 10

For the cream
300ml (10fl oz) double (heavy) cream

100g (3½oz) dark brown sugar

For the cake
230g (8¼oz) butter at room temperature

400g (14oz) caster (superfine) sugar

4 eggs, separated

300g (10oz) desiccated (dried, shredded) coconut

100g (3½oz) plain (all-purpose) flour, sifted

1 tsp baking powder

Zest of 3 oranges, to serve

For the syrup
Juice of 4 oranges

500g (1lb 2oz) caster (superfine) sugar

The brown sugar cream can be made up to a day in advance. Whisk the double (heavy) cream until very thick, gradually adding the brown sugar and whisking well between each addition. Set aside in the refrigerator and serve well chilled.

To make the cake, preheat the oven to 180°C (160°C fan/350°F/Gas 4) and grease and line a 25cm (10in) round deep cake tin. Whisk the butter and sugar together until fluffy using an electric hand whisk (hand mixer), then add the egg yolks, one at a time, whisking to combine between each addition. Set aside.

Whisk the egg whites in a large bowl with a pinch of sugar using an electric hand whisk (ensure both the bowl and beaters are clean and dry or the egg whites won't thicken). Keep whisking until the mixture forms soft peaks and is thick and glossy. Set aside.

Mix the coconut, flour, and baking powder together in a separate bowl.

Fold the sugar and butter mixture into the egg whites with a third of the dry ingredients. Fold carefully so as not to knock too much air out of the egg whites. Add another third of the dry ingredients, fold again to combine, then repeat for the final third.

Pour the batter into the prepared cake tin and bake for 40 minutes or until a skewer inserted into the centre of the cake comes out clean.

Allow the cake to cool completely in the tin, then set aside in the fridge.

To make the syrup pour the orange juice, sugar, and 1.5 litres (2¾ pints) water into a medium size saucepan and place over a high heat. Bring to the boil, stirring continuously to prevent the mixture catching, then immediately reduce the heat to low and simmer gently for 30 minutes, or until the mixture has formed syrup the consistency of thin honey.

To serve, remove the cake from the tin onto a serving plate and pour a little of the hot syrup evenly over the cold cake. Allow the syrup to sink in for a minute or so and then repeat with the remaining syrup. Top with the brown sugar cream and orange zest.

The cake can be stored in the fridge for up to 5 days and the cream for up to 3 days.

Vasina Torta

A cake so special, my nan made a version for my parents' wedding. This recipe does require some effort, and a sugar thermometer, but I promise you it's worth it. It's best to use a 23cm (9in) springform cake tin – line the bottom with baking parchment (parchment paper) and oil the sides to make it easier to remove the cake from the tin. Or bake the cake in any tin you like and simply scoop it out to serve. Stored in the fridge, the meringue should stay fairly firm for up to two days.

SERVES 8

For the cake
5 eggs, separated
80g (2¾oz) caster (superfine) sugar
50g (1¾oz) ground walnuts
1 tbsp plain (all-purpose) flour, sifted
½ tsp cream of tartar

For the buttercream
120ml (4fl oz) full-fat (whole) milk
2 tbsp caster (superfine) sugar
250g (9oz) ground walnuts
4 egg yolks
70g (2¼oz) dark chocolate
Juice and zest of 1 orange
180g (6oz) unsalted butter

For the orange syrup
Juice of 2 oranges
3 tbsp caster (superfine) sugar
Orange slices, to serve

For the meringue
200g (7oz) caster (superfine) sugar
4 egg whites
½ tsp cream of tartar
8g (¼oz) vanilla sugar

Preheat the oven to 200°C (180°C fan/400°F/Gas 6). To make the cake, whisk the egg yolks with the sugar until fluffy. Add the walnuts, flour, and cream of tartar and whisk to combine.

Whisk the egg whites until soft peaks form. Add 4 tbsp of the egg whites to the egg yolk mixture and whisk until smooth.

Add the remaining egg whites to the egg yolk mixture and fold to combine. Pour into a lined 23cm (9in) springform cake tin and bake for 20 minutes or until a knife inserted into the centre comes out clean. Set aside to cool completely before turning out.

To make the buttercream, add the milk and sugar to a small saucepan over a medium heat and bring to the boil. Remove from the heat, add the walnuts, and stir to combine. Set aside to cool.

Add the egg yolks to a bowl set over a saucepan of simmering water. Heat, whisking constantly, for 10–12 minutes or until thickened. Set aside to cool.

Melt the chocolate in the same way, then set aside to cool slightly.

Add the milk and walnut mixture to the egg yolks. Then add the orange juice and zest and cooled chocolate and mix thoroughly to combine. Set aside.

Whisk the butter until fluffy (this will take a few minutes) then add the chocolate mixture. Continue to whisk until fluffy and smooth. Set aside to cool.

Once the cake and buttercream are both cool you can spread the buttercream evenly onto the cake and pop it in the fridge while you work on the meringue and syrup.

To make the syrup, add the orange juice and sugar to a small saucepan over a low heat. Bring to the boil and simmer, without mixing, for 10 minutes or until it has the consistency of runny honey. Set aside.

To make the meringue, add the sugar and 120ml (4fl oz) water to a medium saucepan over a medium heat. Bring to the boil, stirring constantly, until the temperature reaches 115°C (239°F) on a sugar thermometer.

Meanwhile whisk the remaining meringue ingredients together using a mixer or electric hand whisk (hand mixer) until soft peaks form. Aim for the sugar syrup and egg mixture to be ready at the same time.

With the whisk running at maximum speed, slowly pour the sugar syrup into the egg mixture in a thin stream, aiming to pour the syrup as close to the side of the bowl as possible. Continue until stiff, shiny peaks form. Set aside or pop in the fridge until you're ready to serve.

Either spoon the meringue into a piping bag and use to decorate the cake or spread the meringue over the top of the cake. Finish with a drizzle of orange syrup and orange slices.

Photographed on pages 208–209.

Halva Cheesecake

There are so many things I hated as a child and now feel sad I missed out on them for all these years; halva sits firmly in that category. I couldn't understand the happiness felt by the adults as the tub was passed around after dinner, or why they didn't want ice cream like me. I'm now head over heels with the super-sweet paste, and the sesame variety lends itself perfectly to this simple, creamy, no-bake cheesecake.

SERVES 10

For the base

300g (10oz) ginger biscuits
(gingersnaps, or any you fancy)

150g (5½oz) salted butter

100g (3½oz) dark chocolate chips

For the filling

150ml (5fl oz) double (heavy) cream

2 heaped tbsp clotted cream

800g (1¾lb) cream cheese

3 tbsp icing (confectioners') sugar

2 tbsp runny honey

8g (¼oz) vanilla sugar or 1 tbsp
vanilla extract

300g (10oz) halva, crumbled

To serve

Fresh fruit or chocolate sauce,
to serve (optional)

The day before serving, make the biscuit base. Blend the biscuits in a blender or food processor or place into a sealed plastic bag and bash to a fine crumb using a rolling pin.

Add the butter and chocolate chips to a bowl set over a saucepan of simmering water and stir until melted. Add the biscuit crumbs and stir to combine. Spread the mixture onto the bottom of a 25cm (10in) springform cake tin, cover with cling film (plastic wrap) and leave to set in the fridge for at least 3 hours.

To make the filling, whip the double cream until stiff peaks form using a mixer or electric hand whisk (hand mixer). Add the clotted cream, cream cheese, icing sugar, honey, and vanilla and whisk to combine. Add the halva and stir to combine.

Pour the filling over the biscuit base. Dip a butter knife or palette knife into a cup of boiling water and use it to smooth the top of the cheesecake. Cover with cling film and leave to set in the fridge overnight.

To remove the cheesecake from the tin, once again dip a butter knife or palette knife into a cup of boiling water. Use the hot knife to carefully ease the cream filling away from the tin slightly, then open the tin. Use the knife to carefully ease the biscuit base away from the tin.

Serve the cheesecake as it is or top with fresh fruit or chocolate sauce.

Biskvit Torta with Peanut Cream and Honey Butter Caramel

It's such an undemanding process to make this no-bake cake with so many variations, and so much inevitable licking of the spoon. This resilient dessert is made even more opulent here with the addition of sweet cream and sweet caramel. Not only does it last for up to five days in the fridge but it can be wrapped in cling film (plastic wrap) and stored in the freezer to be enjoyed at a later date. The cake will become a little soggier but still delicious over time, and it's always best to eat it the day after baking. You will need a flat tray or serving platter to make this and serve it on (I use a 33 x 23cm/13 x 9in tray).

SERVES 12

For the chocolate cream

4 egg yolks

8g (¼oz) vanilla sugar

120g (4¼oz) plain (all-purpose) flour, sifted

100ml (3½fl oz) milk, plus a splash for the tea

300ml (10fl oz) double (heavy) cream

300g (10oz) dark chocolate

150g (5½oz) butter at room temperature

200g (7oz) icing (confectioners') sugar

200g (7oz) ground walnuts

For the base

3 earl grey tea bags

64 petite beurre biscuits (I like the Ulker brand), plus a few extra in case of breakages

For the peanut cream

100g (3½oz) salted peanuts

250g (9oz) mascarpone

1 tbsp icing (confectioners') sugar

For the honey butter caramel

50g (1¾oz) butter

200g (7oz) runny honey

300ml (10fl oz) double (heavy) cream

Sea salt, to serve (optional)

To make the chocolate cream, whisk the egg yolks and vanilla sugar together using a mixer or electric hand whisk (hand mixer) until light and fluffy. With the whisk running, add the flour and milk and whisk until smooth. Set aside.

Add the cream to a small saucepan over a medium heat and bring to the boil. Break the chocolate into squares and add to the pan, stirring until melted.

Add the cream and chocolate mixture to the egg and flour mixture and stir to combine. Set aside to cool.

Whisk the butter and icing sugar together and add to the cooled chocolate mixture. Add the walnuts, stir to thoroughly combine, and set aside.

Make a strong cup of tea using the earl grey tea bags and 240ml (8fl oz) water. Leave to brew for 10 minutes, then remove the tea bags and add the splash of milk. Set aside to cool completely.

Arrange 16 biscuits on the bottom of a 33 x 23cm (13 x 9in) tray to check the positioning. Dunk each biscuit into the cooled tea to soften a little but remove before they are falling apart. Place back on the tray in the same arrangement.

Reserve some of the chocolate cream to cover the top and sides and spread a quarter of the remainder over the biscuits, taking care not to break

the biscuits (replace any broken ones if necessary). Repeat until you have 4 layers, then cover the top and sides with the reserved chocolate cream.

Dip a butter knife or palette knife into a cup of boiling water and use it to smooth the top of the cake. Refrigerate for at least 8 hours, preferably overnight. You can enjoy the cake as it is or add the toppings.

To make the peanut cream, blend the peanuts to a powder in a blender or food processor, then add the mascarpone and icing sugar and blend again until smooth. Set aside.

To make the caramel, add the butter and honey to a medium non-stick saucepan over a low heat. Heat for 10 minutes or until thickened and darkened in colour.

Pour in the double cream and whisk to combine. Stop whisking, bring to the boil, then immediately remove from the heat. Set aside for 15 minutes or until set.

To serve, slice a big chunk of the cake, add a dollop of peanut cream, and finish with a drizzle of the caramel. Sprinkle with sea salt, if liked.

Photographed on page 214.

Tres Leches Cake

Tres leches means "three milks" in Spanish, and in Spain they might call this cake pastel de leches, or torta de tres leches. It's a light, fluffy sponge that's soaked in three types of milk, all topped up with a creamy, rich caramel.

It's most commonly known as a Latin American cake but from around 2015, it became a huge hit in both Turkey and the Balkans. Why? Well, we love our soap operas, specifically the big hitters from both Mexico and Brazil. So next time you're in a Turkish supermarket and you see glossy, milky slices of light sponge, covered in a deep, reflective caramel, remind yourself that the reason it's there and on so many North Macedonian and Albanian tables is that everyone got hooked on a Brazilian soap opera and were driven mad over the sight of one of the main characters serving it to their guests. Sometimes our food connections come from the sore legacy of occupation, other times from something as ridiculous as an obsession with a telenovela.

This cake keeps for three days in the fridge and can be served with fresh fruit or, if you're feeling wild, extra lashings of cream. Make the cake and get it soaking ahead of time, then once it's in the fridge you can make the caramel.

SERVES 8

For the sponge

12 eggs, separated

6 tsp vegetable oil

200g (7oz) caster (superfine) sugar

300g (10oz) plain (all-purpose) flour, sifted

1 tsp baking powder

7g (¼oz) vanilla sugar or 1 tsp vanilla extract

For the three milks

300ml (10fl oz) double (heavy) cream

150ml (5fl oz) condensed milk

200ml (7fl oz) full-fat (whole) milk

For the caramel

125g (4½oz) brown sugar

15g (½oz) butter

200ml (7fl oz) double (heavy) cream

Pinch of sea salt (optional)

To serve

Pinch of sea salt (optional)

Chopped nuts (optional)

Photographed on page 215.

Preheat the oven to 170°C (150°C fan/325°F/Gas 3). To make the sponge, whisk the egg whites using a mixer or electric hand whisk (hand mixer) until soft peaks form.

In a separate bowl whisk the egg yolks, oil, and sugar together until creamy and fluffy. Fold the egg whites into the egg yolk mixture.

Add the flour, baking powder, and vanilla sugar to a bowl and mix to combine.

Add a third of the dry mixture to the wet mixture, folding carefully to combine but not overmixing. Repeat with the remaining mixtures.

Transfer to a well-greased, deep baking tray approximately 30 x 19cm (12 x 7½in) and bake for 25 minutes or until a knife inserted into the centre comes out clean.

Meanwhile, combine the ingredients for the three milks in a jug (measuring cup).

Use a toothpick or skewer to poke holes evenly over the surface of the sponge and pour over the three milks mixture. Allow to cool, then refrigerate for at least three hours or overnight.

To make the caramel, add the sugar and butter to a small saucepan over a low heat and heat until almost completely melted. Don't be tempted to stir and keep an eye on it to check it doesn't burn. Remove from the heat immediately.

Gradually add the cream, whisking after each addition and until a smooth caramel forms. I like to add a pinch of sea salt at this stage, but this is totally optional.

Remove the cake from the fridge and drizzle with the caramel, spreading it out with a spatula if needed.

Finish with a sprinkle of sea salt or chopped nuts, or serve just as it is and enjoy the simple beauty of the tres leches.

Kadaif Banoffee Pie

Kadaif is a super crunchy, shredded pastry that is usually used in desserts such as knafeh or in baklava, but here it offers a glorious crown to a classic, sweet pie spiked with savoury tahini.

SERVES 8

For the base

12 chocolate digestive biscuits (chocolate graham crackers)

100g (3½oz) unsalted butter, melted

2 tbsp toasted sesame seeds

1 tbsp sesame oil

Pinch of salt

For the caramel

90g (3¼oz) butter

90g (3¼oz) soft dark brown sugar

397g (14oz) tin of condensed milk

3 tbsp tahini

3 ripe bananas, sliced

For the kadaif crown

300–400g (10–14oz) packet of kadaif pastry at room temperature

80g (2¾oz) unsalted butter

4 tbsp runny honey, plus extra to serve

For the cream

800ml (1½ pints) double (heavy) cream

8 tbsp soft brown sugar

8 tbsp tahini

To make the base, blend the biscuits in a blender or food processor or place into a sealed plastic bag and bash to a fine crumb using a rolling pin. Add to a bowl with the melted butter, sesame seeds, sesame oil, and salt and stir to combine. Spread the mixture evenly into the bottom of a 25cm (10in) cake tin, spreading and flattening with a spatula, and chill for 2 hours.

To make the caramel add the butter and sugar to a small saucepan over a low heat and heat until melted. Add the condensed milk, stir to combine, and bring to the boil. Add the tahini and a pinch of salt and continue to boil for 2–3 minutes or until thickened, stirring from time to time to ensure it doesn't catch on the bottom. Pour the mixture over the biscuit base and return to the fridge for a further 2 hours to set.

To make the kadaif crown, preheat the oven to 180°C (160°C fan/350°F/Gas 4). Unwrap the pastry and manipulate into a crown or wreath shape – the pastry can take some manipulating so don't be afraid when handling it.

Add the butter and honey to a large saucepan over a low heat and heat until melted. Stir to combine, then dip the crown into the butter mixture, coating and soaking it as much as possible. Place the crown onto a lined baking sheet and bake for 10 minutes or until golden brown. Set aside to cool.

To make the cream, whip the double cream with the sugar and tahini until soft peaks form.

Remove the pie from the fridge and arrange the banana slices on top of the caramel. Spread half of the cream on top and add the kadaif crown. Finish with the rest of the cream dolloped in the middle, a drizzle of honey and a crushed biscuit.

Tulumbi

Although variations can be found in neighbouring Greece and as far afield as Iran, these little bombs of fried dough in syrup originated in the Ottoman Empire. In the Old Bazaar area of Skopje resides a woman called Dostana, and in her little corner shop she fries her transcendental tulumbi (pronounced "tooloombee"), laying them out next to her husband's baklava.

She moved to North Macedonia in the 70s, closing up her restaurant in Istanbul and starting a new life of dessert making. She lights up when I tell her that I cook for a living, telling me to never let go of that, that I'll never find anything as satisfying. Just like Toni in his kafana (see page 101), Dostana wonders why her three sons, who all work in the law, wouldn't prefer to continue her tradition, her legacy. At least this recipe is a little part of the same fabric as dear Dostana.

You'll need to arm yourself with a piping bag with a large, star-shaped nozzle and a good non-stick saucepan for the dough. If you're making these for the Tulumbi Tiramisu on page 224, you won't need to make the syrup, as the tulumbi will be soaked in the coffee syrup instead.

MAKES ABOUT 24

For the syrup
700g (1½lb) caster (superfine) sugar

Juice of 1 lemon

For the dough
60g (2oz) butter at room temperature

1 tbsp caster (superfine) sugar

125ml (4fl oz) full-fat (whole) milk

½ tsp salt

8g (¼oz) vanilla sugar

230g (8oz) plain (all-purpose) flour, sifted

2 eggs, whisked

About 400ml (14fl oz) vegetable or sunflower oil, for frying

To make the syrup, add the sugar and lemon juice to a small saucepan over a medium heat and bring to the boil, stirring to prevent the sugar from sticking to the bottom of the pan. Boil for 8–10 minutes until a syrup forms. Set aside.

To make the dough, add the butter, sugar, milk, and 250ml (9fl oz) warm water to a large non-stick saucepan over a medium heat and bring to the boil. Stir and remove from the heat.

Mix the salt and vanilla sugar into the flour. Gradually add the flour mixture to the pan with the milk mixture, whisking after each addition, to form a smooth dough. Return to a very low heat and heat, stirring with a spatula, for 2 minutes. Transfer to a mixer or large bowl.

Beat the dough using a mixer or electric hand whisk (hand mixer) for 3–4 minutes, then gradually add the egg, whisking after each addition (the dough will wrap around the whisk so you may need to stop and remove it every so often).

Heat the oil in a large saucepan over a medium-low heat for 8 minutes.

Transfer the dough to a piping bag with a large, star-shaped nozzle and carefully pipe 7.5cm (3in) dough cylinders (or any shape and size you fancy) into the oil from a short height (so that you don't burn yourself), using scissors to cut off the ends. Fry for 2–3 minutes or until golden brown, working in batches as needed and using a slotted spoon to move the tulumbi in the oil so that they cook evenly. Drain briefly on a tea towel or kitchen paper (paper towel) so they are still relatively hot when dropped into the syrup; this will ensure they stay crispy on the outside.

Transfer the tulumbi to the syrup and turn to coat. Leave for 15 minutes, then remove using a slotted spoon and serve.

Tulumbi Tiramisu

Taking inspiration from the usually light Italian dessert, this version uses tulumbi over ladyfinger biscuits which are drenched in a sweet, coffee syrup. It's boozy, decadent and full of mountains of cream – my kind of pudding.

SERVES 6–8

1 quantity Tulumbi (see page 219)

For the coffee syrup
600ml (1 pint) coffee liqueur
3 tbsp instant coffee granules
200g (7oz) caster (superfine) sugar

For the cream
400ml (14fl oz) double (heavy) cream
250g (9oz) mascarpone
2¼ tbsp coffee liqueur

To serve
Cocoa powder
Chocolate shavings

To make the coffee syrup, add all the ingredients and 100ml (3½fl oz) water to a large saucepan over a medium heat. Bring to the boil and cook for 10 minutes or until thickened. Set aside to cool completely.

Soak the tulumbi in the coffee syrup for 15 minutes. Remove from the syrup using a slotted spoon.

Meanwhile, make the cream. Whisk all of the ingredients together using a mixer or electric hand whisk (hand mixer) until stiff peaks form.

To assemble, arrange half of the tulumbi in the bottom of a large serving dish. Top with half of the cream, then layer over the remaining tulumbi and cream. Finish with a sprinkling of cocoa powder and chocolate shavings. Chill for 4–8 hours before serving.

Photographed on pages 222–223.

Cream Cheese Ice Cream

What better way to round off my deep adoration for white cheese than by making an ice cream out of it. Is there anything more divine than an affair between sweet and salty? I used a brined, sheep's milk cheese, but you can use feta, cream cheese, or any other young soft cheese. Use it in the Sour Cherry Baklava Sundae on page 228 or just serve it with a generous drizzle of honey.

Blend the cheese of your choice in a blender or food processor until smooth.

Whip the cream until stiff peaks form using an electric hand whisk (hand mixer). Add the condensed milk and cheese and whisk until combined.

Pour into a freezer-proof container, seal, and freeze. The ice cream will be ready to eat in 24 hours.

MAKES 1.5L (2¾ PINTS)

250g (9oz) full-fat cream cheese, feta, or other soft cheese at room temperature

500ml (16fl oz) double (heavy) cream, well chilled

420ml (14½fl oz) condensed milk

Sour Cherry Baklava

Known in my family as Suze's Baklava, there's no denying that out of the millions of dishes I've had the honour of eating at my auntie's table, this is the one that we all think about, talk about, and request the most. I was given the greatest gift of spending time at her home in Oreshani, a mountain village just outside Skopje. Stepping out onto the balcony, surrounded by deep forest, she laid out her recipe book and the ingredients we needed to make the baklava. The most crucial component to her process is her electric knife – you know, one of those old-school carvers, usually on the cover of retro recipe books, stuck into a heaving turkey. She uses it to precisely cut into her baklava, proudly telling me how long she has had it (since the 80s): "you don't know how many weddings I've carved meat at with this thing". I can't imagine anyone else rocking up to a wedding with an electric knife, just to get the job done for hundreds of hungry guests. Thank you for all that you are and all that you give, Tetka Suze.

Unlike most baklavas, the use of soured cream gives this one a softer texture and fresher taste. Make the syrup a day ahead if you can, as it gives the lemon extra time to infuse.

SERVES 12

For the syrup
200g (7oz) sugar

Juice of 3 lemons

For the filling
4 eggs

200g (7oz) caster (superfine) sugar

300ml (10fl oz) vegetable oil

2 tsp baking powder

200ml (7fl oz) soured cream

800g (1¾lb) filo (phyllo) pastry

500g (1lb 2oz) frozen sour (tart) cherries, defrosted and drained (retain the juice for making the Sour Cherry Baklava Sundae on page 228)

200g (7oz) panko breadcrumbs

The day before serving, make the syrup. Add the sugar, lemon juice, and 400ml (14fl oz) water to a large saucepan over a high heat and bring to the boil, stirring occasionally to make sure that the sugar doesn't stick to the bottom. Reduce the heat to medium and simmer for 25 minutes or until the mixture resembles runny honey. Set aside to cool completely.

Whisk the eggs and sugar together using an electric hand whisk (hand mixer) until fluffy, then slowly add 200ml (7fl oz) of the oil with the whisk running. Gradually add the baking powder and soured cream and continue to whisk for about 10 minutes until really fluffy. Set aside.

Remove the filo pastry from the fridge and lay out onto a chopping board or clean worksurface. Cover with a clean damp tea towel to stop it from drying out (you may need a few to keep the pastry moist as you work).

Thoroughly oil a 30 x 23cm (12 x 9in) baking tray and preheat the oven to 180°C (160°C fan/350°F/Gas 4).

Set aside 8 sheets of filo for the base and crust. Divide the remainder in 2 so that your baklava is the same thickness either side of the filling.

Lay 4 sheets of the retained filo pastry in the bottom of the tray, brushing each with vegetable oil as you go. You may need to trim and fold the pastry as you go to ensure the layers are even.

Add another sheet of pastry and brush with the soured cream mixture. Add another sheet of pastry and then another, so that every other layer is left dry. Repeat until you've used half of the filo sheets, finishing with a sheet of pastry.

Spread the sour cherries evenly over the pastry, adding a little of the juice as you go. Sprinkle over the breadcrumbs.

Repeat the process of one wet, one dry layer using the other half of the pastry. Layer over the 4 remaining sheets of pastry you set aside earlier, brushing each with vegetable oil as you go to form the crust.

If you don't have an electric carving knife to hand dip a sharp knife into a cup of boiling water. Carefully slice the baklava, cutting all the way through, into any portion size or shape you fancy.

Bake for 30–40 minutes or until deep, golden brown. Set aside to cool completely.

Reheat the syrup until just hot (be careful not to let it burn). Pour the syrup all over the baklava, then lift the baking tray up so that it's slanted and allow the syrup to soak into each pastry layer. Repeat on every side of the tray and until you you've used up all of the syrup.

Sour Cherry Baklava Sundae

This recipe is a guide; it's totally up to you if you want to add more baklava, more cream, less syrup, extra nuts, shavings of white chocolate... It's a sundae after all, forever a symbol of joy and the freedom to go wild!

SERVES 4

400ml (14fl oz) sour (tart) cherry juice

1 tbsp caster (superfine) sugar

80g (2¾oz) pistachios, finely chopped

200g (7oz) cherries

200ml (7fl oz) double (heavy) cream

2 tbsp runny honey

8 pieces of Sour Cherry Baklava (see page 226)

8 scoops of Cream Cheese Ice Cream (see page 225) or vanilla ice cream

Ideally make the syrup at least a day in advance (it can be stored in the fridge for up to a month) so it's well chilled before use. Add the sour cherry juice and sugar to a medium saucepan over a medium heat and cook for about 13 minutes or until the mixture has the consistency of honey when cooled (you can test this by popping a teaspoon of the syrup in the fridge for 20 minutes). Set the syrup aside in the fridge.

Place half of the pistachios and the syrup in separate bowls. Dip the cherries in the syrup, coating thoroughly, then roll gently in the nuts to cover. Set aside on a plate in the fridge (this can be done a couple of hours before serving) and retain any leftover syrup and pistachios.

Whip the double cream with the honey until thick, then set aside in the fridge.

To reheat the baklava, preheat the oven to 180°C (160°C fan/350°F/Gas 4). Place the baklava pieces onto a baking sheet, cover with foil, and heat for 10 minutes (you don't need to reheat the baklava but there's something special about the combination of hot and cold in a sundae).

Arrange your sundaes. Go wild or stick with tradition and pile the individual elements into serving bowls. Once you're happy with your arrangement, cover the sundaes with the remaining cherry syrup and pistachio nuts and serve.

Acknowledgments

My dearest Dragica, guardian of this book; you held my hand throughout this whole journey. You gave me the resources I needed to write my story and I am eternally grateful that you came into my life.

Svetlana, my mum, my best friend. You have picked me up countless times, brushed me off, lifted me up, and pushed me along. You are my icon, my hero, and the very meaning of home.

Dad, that little girl you used to stay up all night with singing Patsy Cline songs wrote a book! Thank you for showing me how proud you are of your Dunde.

Suze, you are the most incredible cook. Forever dedicated to hosting and making the best of every ingredient. You gave me the sour cherry baklava and showed me what it means to love.

Uncle Kole, losing you along this journey almost broke me but your boundless pride in me will always carry me through

A huge thank you to Oliver at Oki for providing me with so much joy through burek – the best the city has to offer – and a huge inspiration for my shop.

David, that first visit to your farm inspired this entire story and your warmth and wise words made me realize how important it is to tell. Here's to a lifetime of friendship and an abundance of cheese, good wine, and rock 'n roll.

Toni and Frosina, your dedication to keeping the kafana alive should receive the highest honours. I've never met anyone that works as hard as you two – keep going. Skopje just wouldn't be the same without you.

Slavica, you've always been such a huge part of my life. A dear, sweet soul with a wicked sense of humour. You've shown me the power of being graceful and you make the best musaka in the world.

Natasa, my sister. From our very first meeting the pull between our two souls set us up for a friendship I had only dreamed of. I am seriously proud to know you.

Vera & Jane, opening up your garden gate for us, opened up this book. Your warmth knows no bounds and your preserves are the absolute best.

Baba Slavka, there are still days that I forget you are gone. You are at the very core of everything I do. From the bottom of my heart, I will always love you.

Writing a book while setting up a shop might have been the hardest time of my life – it truly takes a village.

Caitlin, spending all that time with you on my grandmother's balcony in Skopje brought this book to life. The support you have shown me glows through every photograph. Not only are you extremely talented, but your dedication to getting the best out of everything shows your unconditional love and I am so grateful that we got to work together so closely on this book.

To be given the opportunity of a book deal is one thing, but to luck out and work with such an incredible team at DK has eased this emotional and wild experience along the way. Cara, Izzy, Barbara, you have all been so supportive and your excitement over the project has lifted me up along the way. Thanks also to Emma and Georgie for their work on editorial and design.

I wouldn't have got here without Zoe from United Agents seeing something in me, and without Olivia's assistance throughout the process.

Daisy, Valerie, Hanna, Saskia, Susanna; what an absolute dream team and a powerhouse of women. You made the days on set seem easy. Thank you for pouring so much into the work and for also bringing the laughs!

Thank you to all the businesses that hosted me and my food along the way, providing me with a space and a platform to grow over the last few years, taking me in with my burek, and helping me work towards what I have now. And to those that worked alongside me.

A big thank you to my community of customers whose support has taken my baby, my business, to new heights.

My friends, you were all there when I almost snapped, there to voicenote me, text me, drop into the shop, give me a hug, and make sure I never gave up.

My burek family: Verity, Jay, Ostara, and Wolfie. My bestie, Ophie. Bound together since year five, Satnam. My partners in crime, Mrs and Mrs Rooney. The best mum and front of house in the world, Lauren. My queen, Paris Rosina. Marie, where would I have been without our supportive waffles? Tom, Ed, Bea, Jake, Bica, Leanne, LouLou, Hiroko, Mackenzie, Hannha, Eszti, Rachel, Sophie, and all the other wonderful souls I get to know, I know you'll always have my back.

A final thank you to my entire family and my ancestors for shaping me into who I am today.

I love you all!

Index

Note: page numbers in bold refer to images.

About the Author

Spasia Pandora Dinkovski is a London-based chef and writer, and the creator of Mystic Burek. Growing up in West Sussex in the UK, she was encouraged to embrace her Macedonian heritage, learning the language while spending whole summers in North Macedonia with family. Too Balkan to be British, and too British to be Balkan, Spasia found that food was the ultimate way of connecting with both of her homes, and in July 2020 she launched Mystic Burek as a way of further cementing her cultural identity as part of the diaspora. Inspired by a craving for her grandmother's cheese and egg filo pie, Mystic Burek started as a delivery service of traditional North Macedonian-style pastries and Balkan snacks across London, before expanding into event catering and endlessly popular pop-up events. In September 2023 the Mystic Burek shop, a small Balkan haven serving traditional bureks made with contemporary and local ingredients, opened in Sydenham, London. An experienced chef with 15 years in professional kitchens in London and New York, Spasia was voted one of the *Observer Food Monthly* magazine's "50 things we love in the world of food". She has featured in *The Times*, *Olive* magazine, *Time Out,* the *Telegraph,* and the *Guardian*. *Doma*, meaning "home" is Spasia's first book.

Publisher's Acknowledgments

DK would like to thank Sarah Epton for proofreading, Lisa Footitt for the index, and Adam Brackenbury for the image retouching. Thanks also to Hanna Miller and Susanna Unsworth for their assistance on food styling, and to Coco Bagley, Matilda Norris, and Oliver Goodrich for their assistance on photography.

Picture Credits

The publisher would like to thank the following for their kind permission to reproduce their photographs:

(Key: a-above; b-below/bottom; c-center; f-far; l-left; r-right; t-top)

All images photographed by Caitlin Isola apart from:

Verity Quirk: 238; **Spasia Pandora Dinkovski:** 25bl, 92t, 92b, 117, 143, 172, 177, 185, 201tl, 201tr, 202, 202cr, 203bl, 225, 230tc, 230tr, 230bc, 231br

Cover images: Caitlin Isola

All other images © Dorling Kindersley

Cook's Note

The recipes in this book are presented in British English with translated terms in parentheses for US readers. Some exceptions and their explanations: "Runny honey" is commonly known as simply "honey" in the US. Pork scratchings are a packaged snack similar to pork rinds. A "barbecue" is commonly called a "grill" in the US, whereas a "grill" is called a "broiler." Also note that many ingredients are given by weight, which increases precision. An inexpensive kitchen scale is required to get the most from the recipes.

DK | Penguin Random House

Editorial Director Cara Armstrong
Project Editor Izzy Holton
Senior Designer Barbara Zuniga
Production Editor David Almond
Senior Production Controller Samantha Cross
Jacket and Sales Material Coordinator Emily Cannings
DTP and Design Coordinator Heather Blagden
Editorial Manager Ruth O'Rourke
Art Director Maxine Pedliham
Publishing Director Katie Cowan

Editorial Emma Bastow
Design Georgie Hewitt
Photography Caitlin Isola
Prop styling Daisy Shayler-Webb, Luis Peral
Food styling Saskia Sidey, Valerie Berry

First American Edition, 2024
Published in the United States by DK Publishing
1745 Broadway, 20th Floor, New York, NY 10019

A catalog record for this book is available from the Library of Congress.
ISBN 978-0-7440-9246-2

Printed and bound in China

www.dk.com

MIX
Paper | Supporting responsible forestry
FSC™ C018179

This book was made with Forest Stewardship Council™ certified paper - one small step in DK's commitment to a sustainable future.
For more information go to www.dk.com/our-green-pledge